UNION

UNION

ENCOUNTERING JESUS IN
LIFE LIVED TOGETHER

MATT BRADWAY

Unless otherwise noted, all Scripture quotations are taken from the Holy Bible, New Living Translation, copyright ©1996, 2004, 2015 by Tyndale House Foundation. Used by permission of Tyndale House Publishers, a Division of Tyndale House Ministries, Carol Stream, Illinois 60188. All rights reserved.

Scripture quotations marked (ESV) are taken from The ESV® Bible (The Holy Bible, English Standard Version®), © 2001 by Crossway, a publishing ministry of Good News Publishers. Used by permission. All rights reserved.

Scripture quotations marked (CSB) have been taken from the Christian Standard Bible®, Copyright © 2017 by Holman Bible Publishers. Used by permission. Christian Standard Bible® and CSB® are federally registered trademarks of Holman Bible Publishers.

Edited by Abbey McLaughlin
Cover design and interior formatting by Damonza

ISBN (Paperback): 979-8-9996197-0-9
ISBN (Hardback): 979-8-9996197-1-6
ISBN (eBook): 979-8-9996197-2-3

For Mama.

Thank you for showing me that it's ok to raise
your hands in church.

CONTENTS

Prologue: Breath. 1

Part One: Experience. 12

    Chapter 1: Pictures 15

    Chapter 2: Yada (Part 1) 33

    Chapter 3: Yada (Part 2) 55

    Chapter 4: Bridges 79

Part Two: Character 98

    Chapter 5: Name. 101

    Chapter 6: Womb 109

    Chapter 7: Running. 135

    Chapter 8: Restore. 157

    Chapter 9: Bound 185

    Chapter 10: Sunshine 211

Part Three: Together 238

    Chapter 11: Family 241

    Epilogue: Lyrics 269

Appendix: Home Church Rule of Life 279

A Note from Matt 283

The Union Community 285

Thank You 286

About the Author. 288

BREATH

WHEN PEOPLE ASK me what it's like to be a professional pilot, I usually tell them it's ninety-eight percent boredom and two percent sheer terror.

For the vast majority of the time, I just sit there and watch the clouds go by. I sip watered-down airline coffee and savor the flavor of chemical sanitizers mixed with cheap Arabica beans. I do crosswords. I think. Yes, piloting a flying bus is largely a mundane endeavor, but not all the time. There is a small red square light positioned on the control panel right between my eyes. If that light were to start flashing and the alarm bells were to start ringing, that means, among other things, that my flight is no longer boring.

There's a host of things that can go wrong while flying, from engine fires to computer glitches, flight control malfunctions to stuck landing gear. As aircraft have become more complex, so have the number of possible problems. Don't worry—I'm prepared for this. Every year, I get thrown into a simulator where they basically try to kill you for a week straight with various malfunctions in order to expose pilots to literally any possible threat.

I am proud to report, I haven't died in a simulator yet.

One of the more dangerous yet indistinct problems an airplane can experience has to do with cabin pressure. Way up at the altitudes airliners cruise at, there's not a whole lot of oxygen to breathe. Airplanes are pressurized with air to allow for flight at those high altitudes. And if the airplane were to suddenly lose cabin pressure, oxygen masks fall from the ceiling, providing an emergency supply of oxygen until the aircraft can descend to a safer, lower altitude.

Up where the pilots sit, we are trained to do nothing until we get our own oxygen masks on. In fact, many airplanes have pilot oxygen masks designed to be put on within five seconds using only one hand. Speed is incredibly important here. Nothing else matters except getting the oxygen flowing to your lungs again.

At 35,000 feet, you have about thirty seconds left of consciousness should the airplane suddenly lose cabin pressure. But while it's certainly possible that cabin pressure can be lost instantaneously, a more likely scenario is that the oxygen in the airplane will decrease over time due to a slow leak. The reason that loss of cabin pressure is so dangerous is because it can be quite subtle. If an airplane slowly loses cabin pressure, chances are you wouldn't notice anything until it was too late.

Losing consciousness due to lack of oxygen doesn't happen all at once. Over time, you start to lose awareness of your surroundings as your vision starts to narrow. You might begin to feel dizzy, unable to react, to think, or to speak clearly. The process happens over time until you become lifeless. As the air gets progressively thinner, sleepiness sets in and you might feel a little nauseous, until you just close your eyes and go to sleep…but you wouldn't wake up.

It's the subtlety that kills you. The slow dimming of awareness, the gradual descent into deeper and deeper realms of disorientation. You don't feel in danger until you are beyond recovery. By the time you realize what's happening, you don't have the strength or cognition to pull yourself out.

Well, so much for starting this book off on a happy note. Obviously, planes have numerous protections in place to account for small leaks as well as to detect them—and oxygen masks to save us if we sense something is wrong. My point is that small changes over a long period of time are almost unrecognizable in the moment. We want to stop and assess ourselves and our surroundings often enough to know if we need an oxygen mask, and we're not naturally designed to notice small changes in the moment, so it takes work. So it is with breathing, and so it is with life following Jesus.

If we aren't aware of these tiny little changes, if we don't keep our eyes on our lives and who we are becoming, we can *drift*—to depart from our original intentions, to settle into a new way of living and call it "just the way things are." What we need are warning lights in our minds and hearts to wake us up and snap us back to reality. We should want these moments of clarity; we should desire them. I don't *want* the alarm bells to go off in my airplane, but I'm thankful that they *will* if the situation calls for it.

This book is an invitation into a moment of clarity. It's a chance to pause, to take an honest look at your relationship with Jesus, and ask yourself two questions:

1. Am I living the kind of life Jesus intends for me to live?
2. Am I experiencing the kind of life Jesus intends for me to experience?

Jesus intends for you to know him in a way that feels vibrant, flourishing, intimate, and deep. Is this your experience? Have your senses that used to pick up on his love become dulled and unresponsive? Has your life of faith slowly changed into something pedestrian, routine, or flat? Do you long for more of *something*, even if you can't quite put your finger on it?

If that's you, you've picked up the right book.

When we neglect our *relationship* with Jesus, we experience a spiritual loss of consciousness. It's subtle, just like losing cabin pressure in an airplane. It might start with a "dry season" in our faith that stretches from a few weeks to a few months, maybe even into a couple of years or decades. Slowly, our sense of the Holy Spirit can become dull, worship can feel lifeless or manufactured, and the affections we once felt for Jesus might start to be replaced with a dutiful, joyless obedience. The easy, beautiful rhythm of life with Jesus starts to feel like a heavy, bothersome burden that we just can't shake. We find ourselves out of breath, out of strength, out of life. Some of us may wonder where it all went wrong. Others might just be ready to throw in the towel and move on. The temptation to just shut our spiritual eyes and give in to the heaviness is all too real.

The relational component of our faith and trust in Jesus is where many of us started to experience that spiritual oxygen leak. We are asked to dig deeper into Jesus than just studying him. Jesus says that real, eternal life is *knowing him*. That's why we don't experience this real, vibrant, oxygen-rich life today.

We don't know what it means to know God.

John 17 contains what many people consider to be Jesus' "High Priestly Prayer." In the Old Testament, the primary job of the High Priest was to go before God and intercede on behalf of the people. Here we see Jesus doing the same thing, praying to God first for himself, then his disciples, and then for everyone else who would come after his disciples by faith in him.

In case you're wondering, yes, that includes you. *Specifically you.*

So here is Jesus, looking up into the sky, praying this for *you*:

> *This is eternal life: that they may know you, the only true God, and the one you have sent—Jesus Christ.* (John 17:3 CSB)

Simply put, Jesus is praying that you would *know him*.

Notice the reason he's praying this. *Knowing him is what leads to life.*

Knowing Jesus leads to *real* life for today. There is a "here and now" aspect to our knowledge of the creator. Today, the life we experience and the life other people experience from us originates in our felt relationship with Jesus. The closer we live to the source of life, the purer our lives will be, and this is good for us and for those around us.

I live in Minneapolis, which sits on the banks of the mighty Mississippi River. The source of the river is Lake Itasca in northern Minnesota. Lake Itasca itself is very clean, with water that's so clear you can see to the bottom of the lake. As the Mississippi flows south though, the water becomes progressively dirtier as the silt and pollutants from the surrounding land seep into the river.

At the Gulf of Mexico, where the Mississippi ends, there is actually a "dead zone," which prevents any aquatic life from existing due to the level of contaminants in the river. The clear, life-giving water of Lake Itasca turns poisonous. The farther the river gets from its source, the more contaminated and polluted it becomes until the clean waters of Itasca become unrecognizable.

Your relationship with God is the headwaters of your life. It affects everything about you, from how you think, to how you feel, to how you act. The state of your relationship with God touches all of your reality. This is why Jesus links knowing him to *real* life. If our sense of relationship with God is strong, we'll feel more like a life-giving river because we are living closer to the source of life. If we disregard our knowing of God, our lives will become progressively muddied and our spirits will feel more like a "dead zone." This will cause us to think, feel, and act in ways that are contrary to our God-given identity. We'll end up unable to feel much of anything, either from ourselves or God. We'll start believing the lies that shame tells us, that we are unlovable, beyond rescue, and that God is wasting his time.

Knowing Jesus leads to experiencing a full, vibrant life today. But it's also linked to our eternal destinies.

"Eternal life" in the John 17 passage—promised to believers in

John 3:16 and elsewhere—is all about our heavenly lives. Eternal life is not found in good behavior. You won't spend eternity with Jesus because of your stellar church attendance record. No amount of volunteering, helping the poor, hours spent singing songs of worship, or asking Jesus into your heart will restore your relationship to your creator.

The people who will spend their eternities with Jesus are the ones who *know* him. Your eternal destiny is linked to your relationship with God. So yeah, this is kind of important.

We can read all the books, listen to all the sermons, and do all the self-reflection, but the fact remains that unless we deal with the headwaters of who we are as people, our relationship with our creator, we'll just be spinning our wheels.

Knowing about God and knowing God are two very different things. I would argue that they are eternally different. Jesus' prayer above is not a prayer that you would simply increase in your knowledge of God. Jesus' prayer for you is that you would find an authentic *relationship* with God, moving past *awareness* of who he is and into a regular *encountering* of him as a living, dynamic being. True knowledge of God is *felt, experienced relationship with him*, just like the relationships you have with other people.

I'm writing this book to myself, fifteen years ago. Back then, I was a follower of Jesus, but behind the activity of being a Christian, I was incredibly dissatisfied with my experience of the Christian life. I had always believed in Jesus, but the life that he was giving me felt conventional, pedestrian, and forced. I looked across the landscape of the American church and found myself apologizing for her more than serving her. I became disillusioned and distracted, the once vibrant colors of my faith slowly fading. I just wanted to *feel* something.

The most haunting part of that season of life was that *I was fine with it.* I was at peace with my feelings of dissatisfaction. A frustrating, uninspired life of faith was *normalized.* I was getting lulled to sleep, and I was happy to close my eyes.

I was drifting away. And I was content.

In 2012, God sounded the alarm bells and dropped an oxygen mask for me—a series of events that forced me to confront the reality of my lifeless connection to the supposed giver of life.

Our first child was born with physical complications that tested my belief in a God that loved me. If God decided to allow me to experience a physical difference, I would have been okay. But when it came to my child, God seemed to have crossed a line.

A few years later, we spent an afternoon praying and visiting with some dear friends of ours just before they left with their children to serve Jesus in Japan. A week later they were rear ended on a highway by a semi-truck going eighty miles an hour. This challenged my belief in a God who was good.

My wife and I suffered through a miscarriage which led me to doubt in a God who was powerful and who supposedly knit babies together in the womb. Why was our baby an exception, God?

My mother, who was the greatest spiritual influence in my life, collapsed at the front door of my childhood home from a heart attack and struggled in a hospital bed for three weeks before dying, which caused me to question my belief in a God who heals.

I was unexpectedly laid off from my job as an airline pilot, which made me reevaluate my belief in a God who provides.

Knowing about God wasn't enough. Simply being aware that he existed out there somewhere wasn't enough. My theological understanding of God's love, goodness, power, ability to heal, and provision wasn't able to sustain my faith. What I needed was a relationship with him. During those trying years, *God used his people* to love me back into experiencing the love of Jesus. In a million mundane little encounters with the family of God, I was gently guided back into knowing him again. The family of God became a place where I could gently lay down my pain, questions, and doubts and receive compassion, love, and truth. God's family provided the tangible experiences I needed to reignite my faith and renew my relationship with him.

God used his people to guide this content drifter back home.

Let me tell you a wonderful truth: *Jesus still walks the earth today.* He does this through his Holy Spirit living inside his people. When we encounter the united family of God walking according to the Spirit, we encounter Jesus himself. Sometimes, I feel the comfort of Jesus in the solitude of a morning prayer walk. Other times, I feel it in the taste of a smoked brisket from my brother Eric when even the thought of planning dinner was too much.

Sometimes, I feel the love of Jesus while reading the book of Romans. Other times, I feel his love when I find my friend Brendan in my house at five a.m. installing flooring for me when my life was already overflowing with worries and things to do.

Sometimes, I feel the strength of Jesus in a timely sermon or worship song. Other times, I feel his strength when my neighbor Noah hears of all the frustrations I am holding and demands that I come over to his house to pray over me while he's doing the dishes.

Where is Jesus today? He's found walking among his people. By devoting ourselves to the family of Jesus, we will grow in our relationship with Jesus himself. We will experience our *union* with Christ. To be in union with someone means to have your life so intertwined with theirs that you start to take on their qualities, feel how they would feel, and act how they would act. Union is a sacred closeness, an intimate relationship, a weaving together of two different lives into one. To feel in your bones and heart that Jesus is yours, and you are his (Song of Solomon 2:16).

The central claim of this book is this: *The way we can experience the kind of deep union with Jesus that he intends for us is by devoting ourselves to living like family with his people.*

Part One is all about working through our preconceived notions regarding relationship with Jesus and rediscovering what the Bible has to say about knowing God, which includes both knowing him *and* being known by him.

In Part Two, we uncover the attributes God wants us to know about himself and how living like a spiritual family with other people can bring us into those experiences.

Finally, Part Three is meant to be a practical, encouraging roadmap for creating and cultivating your own spiritual family by discovering the three movements of union and how to live those out for the glory of God, the unity of the church, and the redemption of the world.

This book is for the unsatisfied. It's for the longing saints dreaming of breaking into uncharted territory with Jesus. It's for the burnt-out, tired-out, down-and-out children of God who just want to feel something again. It's for those who silently wonder if the church in the west has lost the plot, if we have been prioritizing the wrong things, and who wonder if we have made belonging to the family of God way too complicated.

I wrote this book for the ones who have kept themselves from the risky, vulnerable love of God because of real, tangible pain. These pages are for the ones from broken family backgrounds that have caused the warm, bright rays of Christ's love for them to dim and bend into something unrecognizable. It's for the people who because of hurt, shame, and broken models of relationship experience the Bible's description of God's love more like a funhouse mirror, with visions distorted and strange, foreign and inaccessible.

I wrote this book for you, living your beautiful, normal life as an invitation into the deep life of Jesus that comes by knowing others and being known by them.

It's time to snap back to reality and breathe deep again, to get the oxygen flowing back into our hearts and spirits. It's time to trek uphill, back to the headwaters of our faith, where the water is crystal clear and full of life. It's time to recenter ourselves on what it truly means to know Jesus, the great lover of our souls.

By pursuing union with his people, we experience the reality of our union with Christ.

Take a deep breath. Let's begin.

PART ONE

EXPERIENCE

But those who wish to boast
should boast in this alone:

that they truly know me.

(JEREMIAH 9:24A)

CHAPTER 1

PICTURES

I was voted "best dressed" in high school. Not bad for a gangly, 6'6", 170 pounds soaking wet, introverted mega-nerd. Argyle sweaters with skinny jeans were my weapon of choice, and I was a stone-cold killer. I grew my hair long, down to my shoulders, and every morning I would violently rub my hair into a giant, frizzy, unruly mess. I would then empty about a half a can of Aussie Instant Freeze hairspray onto it, which froze it into a sticky, smelly mass.

I can still smell that hairspray.

Ever since I can remember, I've wanted to be different. I wanted people to notice me and think, "Wow, that Matt guy is so cool, so edgy, so mysterious." That desire hit its fever pitch in high school, but I still carry it with me today. As I've gotten older and done more processing of my past, I've realized that my desire to be different was not random. It came from somewhere.

That somewhere was my mother.

My mother, Carolyn Bradway, developed a bad case of rheumatoid arthritis when she was a teenager. Rheumatoid arthritis is an autoimmune disease that causes the body's immune system to attack its own joints. If left untreated, joints can lock in place, leading to a lifetime of pain and obvious physical differences.

When she first showed symptoms of RA, there was no effective treatment, so over time, the joints in her arms froze into place. Her elbows fused at almost a ninety-degree angle, and her finger joints locked up in every possible direction. She felt (and looked) different, and that was hard.

I remember going to the grocery store and hearing people call her a "witch."

I remember the constant stares and whispers, the finger-pointing, and curious looks.

I remember the embarrassment I felt in church when she would raise her crooked arms as high as she could in worship to God. I remember my face getting red and sinking deep into the cloth bench.

So little eight-year-old Matt had a choice: continue to avoid the awkwardness and embarrassment of being in public with my own mother, or embrace being a different kind of family, with a different kind of parent, and go full-speed into unapologetically living into that difference. I chose the second option. If they were gonna stare, then might as well give 'em something to stare at.

And from that point on, I was proud to be different. I wanted to make people feel uncomfortable. I wanted to express my individuality, so I walked confidently out of that Maple Grove Target with bags of hairspray and skinny jeans, the blue and green diamonds on my sweater cutting through the beige reality of my actual life.

I felt different, but I wasn't original. My personality was a product of my past, of my specific environment, which is a practically universal experience. Nobody is an original. Your past and your cultural environment have a massive impact on how you act, think, and live.

Only recently have we started to discover just how much our childhood environment affects how we function as adults. Those childhood years, especially from birth to age three, are incredibly impactful. We truly are products of our past. My mom's visible differences made hyper-individuality a protective measure, a coping strategy, for how she was treated differently.

My home life contributed greatly to my identity, but many factors played into it (and still do). In addition to our personal pasts, the cultural environment we live in has a major effect on how we view the world. There are parts of modern culture that operate like a toxic gas we can't escape. We are simmering in the flavors of the world around us. Many of our "default" thoughts and actions are borrowed from our cultural norms.

I'm a Minnesotan, which means I will wear shorts and a t-shirt outside on the first day of the year that it reaches fifty degrees.

I was raised in an upper-middle-class suburban context which means that I learned (and have been unlearning) that college is the only acceptable option after high school.

I grew up in a family that valued frugality and saving money, so I have a hard time ordering anything besides water when I go out to eat.

The point is, we all have thoughts and actions that, to us, feel like the default option for all of humanity. The reality is that we hold them simply because we were conditioned by our environment to hold them.

Part of my initial resistance to starting a house church was my underlying belief that Americans do everything the best way (please don't laugh at my naivety). I assumed that in America, we were on the cutting edge of everything from government and medicine to war and online shopping. This belief came from my cultural upbringing that emphasized the "specialness" of America. We said the pledge of allegiance every day, had days off of school for things like President's Day, and literally blew things up on July 4th to celebrate our great nation.

When my friend Eric approached me about the potential of starting a house church, I laughed and said that was the stupidest idea I had ever heard. In America, big-sanctuary churches with huge parking lots were clearly "church," and America *must* be doing "church" the best way. I mean, just look at those huge displays and the high-energy worship "experiences" inside them. There is no room to innovate because in 'Merica we are the model church for the rest of the world.

I can hear you laughing...

American exceptionalism is baked right into our culture. It shaped the way I viewed the world and consequently, the idea of church. That's just one of the many assumptions we carry in the west that affects our logic and emotions even when we are unaware.

In Christ, you're a new person in an old body. In Christ, you're free yet still influenced by the culture around you. These two forces affect everything about you, from your tolerance level for getting lost on the way to the airport, your personality traits, if you floss every day, cow milk or almond, the place you live, the list can go on forever.

Your personal past and the cultural environment even have an effect on *your concept of what it actually means to have a relationship with God.*

If you grew up with an absent father who only came around to punish you, your concept of God as a good father will be negatively affected. If you were formed in a culture that emphasized strength over weakness, your concept of a murdered Savior will be harder to understand.

So in our endeavor to return to the headwaters of relationship with God, we need to cut a path through the dense brush of all the things hidden in our minds and hearts that affect our default thoughts about God. Let's start out by asking one basic and very loaded question:

What does it mean to know someone?

Every year, our family puts on a Halloween party for the neighborhood. We make large amounts of wild rice soup, homemade sourdough bread, and hot apple cider for anyone and everyone to come by and enjoy. Naturally, this event attracts people from multiple circles of relationship. We have some friends stop by who are from our church, some are family from out of town, and some are neighbor friends we've had for a while. When people from multiple circles all get together in one place, lots of introductions take place.

When I introduce friends from different areas of my life, I make sure to emphasize *experience* over *information* as the linking bridge to making that introduction. For example, if I connect a friend from church with a friend from the neighborhood who don't know each other, I lead with how I know each person and what experiences we all might have in common (children, work, favorite hobbies, etc.).

"Hey Michael! This is Dwight. We both love paintball and the art of beet farming."

That's a lot easier to work with than,

"Hey Michael! This is Dwight. He is wearing a beige dress shirt with a yellow-striped tie."

If someone were to ask me about my wife, I wouldn't start by stating she's thirty-six years old, 5'9", and a human female. I would go on about how we've been married for sixteen wonderful years, and how I love the way she advocates for children with broken family situations. I could also tell the story about the time she called another man "babe" on a hiking trail when she thought it was me. Ya know, all the experiential relationship stuff.

Knowing God is dependent on how you view him. What has been your experience with God? Perhaps you come from a personal and/or cultural background that elevates feeling as the ultimate litmus test for experiencing God. Other people, like my wife, come from a background that elevated the traditions of the church as the primary gateway to knowing God. Some may emphasize the god found in nature or the god found inside us as the true experience of the divine. Still others may reject the idea of experiencing god at all. We may be coming from different backgrounds, but there are two truths here that you and I have in common:

1. Living in the cultural west has an effect on how we approach the concept of knowing God in ways we may not even realize.

2. The Bible has a lot to say on the matter, which is something we can all benefit from.

We all have histories that impact how we view "knowing" our creator. Whatever your personal or culturally conditioned approach to knowing God is, I've got something here for you. Let's read on.

The way people in the world think about knowing God today is a direct result of some pretty major developments throughout history. I'll try to make it brief, but this information will greatly help us as we navigate our own personal and cultural biases we are bringing to the table. What follows is a brief outline on how cultural conditions have historically influenced our idea of knowing God, and why today, *information tends to eclipse experience* as the default vehicle for relationship with God.

I am not an expert in this. Our expert in this endeavor is the Canadian philosopher, Charles Taylor. In 2007, he published a massive book called *A Secular Age,* which investigates some of the very concepts we are wrestling with in this chapter. Taylor's work is incredibly important in our quest to understand our approach to knowing God, and much of the following summary is based on his thoughts.

Taylor's investigation begins in the Middle Ages (roughly 500-1500 AD). During this time period, people had strong interactions with the spiritual they believed were real and tangible. The world was assumed to be filled with, and controlled by, legions of spirits, demons, and forces beyond our control. Everything had a spiritual connection: from sickness, to why your crops failed, to how many kids you had and how long they lived. Taylor calls this assumed, universal, tangible feeling *enchantment,* and people lived in an enchanted world. The spiritual dimension was assumed to be not only real, but the realest thing there was. Atheism was unthinkable.

God's existence seemed as obvious as the sunrise. All of life was saturated with the divine, as God was "sustaining all things by his powerful word" (Hebrews 1:3 CSB). Literally. For many in the Middle Ages, God's existence was an obvious fact and necessary to survive. The world was scary, full of evil spirits looking to harm you. The battle between good and evil was a daily experience, with the evil spirits of "black magic" doing battle against the church, her angels, and her saints. People ran to the church for protection against dark spiritual forces. If you lived back then, this cosmic (and worldly) battle between good and evil spirits would have been the topic of conversation around the dinner table.

Some people were so scared of the power of the communion elements that they had to be *forced* to take it at least once a year.

Can you imagine? *Trembling* as the bread and wine was passed around? Can you imagine feeling so deeply that God was right there, all around you, interacting with you on a daily basis, as close as the breath in your lungs?

Back then knowing God meant interacting with him as their source of survival. He wasn't an afterthought, but the very center of their existence. Their spiritual protection and general wellbeing depended on it. Knowing God meant feeling incredibly vulnerable to his power and trusting him to spiritually intervene in ways only he could do so.

He was real, reachable, knowable, and involved in their lives and world. They would suffer real consequences if they were lazy in their pursuit of him.

This doesn't mean that the Middle Ages were a sort of "golden era" for relationship with God. I am not advocating for a return to 1517. Yes, it's true that experiencing God was much more ingrained and assumed in the day-to-day lives of people, but true relationship with him was still not a guarantee. It's like seeing a police officer with a speed gun and feeling anxious. We feel anxious, but that doesn't mean we have a relationship. You experience him because he is *there,* not because you *know him.* Such was life with God in the Middle Ages. God was *there,* but that didn't mean people *knew him.* Even though the *effects* of God were felt, it was still a struggle to be in *relationship* with him, like it always has been.

The enchanted world of the Middle Ages was the default option for much of humanity, until the sixteenth century.

In the sixteenth century, scientific discovery took off. What started as a theological pursuit to understand God and his world turned into the very thing that would challenge his existence. Using our own intelligence, humans "grew up" and started to discover the world God created for themselves, using their own brains.

And we got pretty good at discovering stuff.

God's truth revealed in Scripture was surpassed by something called *rationalism*, or the belief that humans and their reasonings were the ultimate source of knowledge and truth. With rationalism as the ultimate source of knowledge, humans were primed to discover their world in ways they never had before. The hood of the world's inner workings was popped open. Humans probed and questioned, tested and verified.

In 1522, the Magellan-Elcano exploration finished, becoming the first expedition to sail around the world, thereby proving that it was round and not flat like many people of the Middle Ages had come to believe.

In 1676, Antoni van Leeuwenhoek discovered bacteria. Step aside evil spirits, we now know the real reason for that leprosy.

Maybe it's time to rewrite this exchange in John 9:1-3:

> *As Jesus was walking along, he saw a man who had been blind from birth.*
>
> *"Rabbi," his disciples asked him, "why was this man born blind? Was it because of his own sins or his parents' sins?"*

"It was not because of his sins or his parents' sins," Jesus answered. "~~This happened so the power of God could be seen in him~~ but because of an in-utero genetic mutation in which one of 27 possible genes changed its DNA code, which resulted in the child's blind condition."

Is that better?

All of these discoveries started to give humans the general feeling that the world was not as unknown or scary as they had come to believe. The enchanted world of the Middle Ages started to feel more and more childish and strange. Much like a child scared of a monster under the bed, the scientific revolution "turned on the lights" of the universe and looked under the bed.

They found no monster. Nor did they find a God.

The supernatural mystery of the world has been taken away, and we now dwell in what Taylor calls an *immanent frame*, which sees our lives as operating within a totally natural order, with nothing supernatural going on.

Taylor argues that the events described above opened the door for a new way to think about reality and our place in it: *exclusive humanism*. Simply put, humans are now able to account for their meaning and purpose without any influence from the divine. This was a departure from the thought process of the Middle Ages, wherein humans found more of their meaning and purpose from the divine because God and his influence was unable to be ignored. God was intertwined with every part of their lives, thus their meaning and purpose was to acknowledge that fact in all their daily lives.

Exclusive humanism kicked God out of the house, so our purpose as humans needed to find a new place to stay.

As humanity's view on God shifted from a felt awareness to impersonal existence, we shifted our focus from our hearts to our brains. Feeling is out, thinking is in. The heart is secondary; the brain is ultimate. As the famous enlightenment philosopher Rene Descartes put it, humans are now *Res Cogitans,* or "thinking things." We think, therefore we are. God is out, we are in. There didn't seem to be a need to "know God" anymore.

This doesn't mean that God doesn't exist though; it just means that he didn't really do much in the perspective of the everyday person. He was perceived as just kind of up there, watching us, intervening sometimes. Present, but not a factor. Some of you may be familiar with the term *deism.* That's it.

If God is there, he's only really concerned with our happiness and flourishing. Taylor calls this kind of deism *providential deism.* We aren't ready to do away with God altogether. We still will throw up a few halfhearted prayers every now and again. We'll say "hi" to him at Christmas and Easter, and we'll pray at funerals.

On our historical tour of knowing God, we have now arrived at our present age.

Probably even more applicable to our knowledge journey is the concept of what Taylor calls *the impersonal order.* Remember, we've gotten really good at making discoveries and finding cold, hard facts about the world. What ends up happening as humans try to reconcile a still-existing God and an ever-increasing knowledge of reality is an attempt to help these two diverging thoughts remain in harmony.

Interestingly, we are trying to keep God around while knowing a lot of stuff that seems to make him obsolete. It's almost like humanity just can't let go of the idea of a God. We can't get away from this longing that there's got to be more to life than what we can see. See Ecclesiastes 3:11.

The impersonal order states that God is still there, and he created the world to abide by universal, unchanging laws, which humans have to conform to or suffer the consequences. *So God is still interacting with us, but not dynamically or as "in our face" as we once believed.* He interacts with us as we discover and bump up against his rules that govern the universe.

Go ahead and read that last section again.

To put it another way, we interact with God no longer as a dynamic being who interacts with us as we live our lives, but more like a *concept to be discovered.* We have stripped God of his capacity for relationship (experiencing and being experienced) and thus, view him more as a *concept to be known* about rather than a relational being to be *in relationship with.* Our definition of knowing God has changed from mostly knowing him experientially (pre-sixteenth century) to mostly knowing things about him (post-sixteenth century). This is where we find ourselves today.

We've confused being aware of who God is and how he works for knowing God relationally. It's like we know the measurements of God's dimensions, we can describe how he looks, what he does, and how he thinks, but we have no idea how to relate to him as a living being.

This dynamic reminds me of an ultrasound of a baby. The technician can tell the parents everything about that little person, including how big their head is, to the length of their big toe. Sometimes the parents even get a 3D picture of their face if they're lucky. It's incredible. At the end of the exam, they'll even give the parents a little picture of the baby to take home and hang on the fridge.

I gotta confess here though: Every time I've left that appointment, I feel the same as I did when I first entered that clinic building. Pictures are cool, measurements are interesting, but they aren't my child. You could tell me all you want about what fruit or vegetable most represents the size of my baby, but in the end, it will all fall flat. Data about my child just doesn't do anything for me.

I learned to take a big, deep breath right before I held our newborn children for the first time because I will be unable to breathe for around twenty seconds. When I actually got to hold my daughter, when my eyes met her beet-red, screaming face and clenched fists, I was so overcome with emotion that I couldn't do anything except *exist.* In that moment, she was no longer numbers in a data table or images on photo paper, she became a *real person.*

I was no longer simply aware that my daughter existed. I was experiencing her real presence, and she was experiencing mine. The moment she was born was the moment we started knowing each other.

Pictures are great, but they are no substitute for the real person. Perhaps you have pictures of people you love hanging up in your house or saved onto your phone. Maybe those people have left this earth, or maybe they are just far away. The pictures you have of them are not actually them, though, and some days those feelings are all too real. Maybe you feel the same way about God. Maybe ultrasound pictures of God have been enough for you instead of being in his presence.

This is why for some of us, we feel a vague, uneasy dissatisfaction with our relationship with God that's kind of hard to put a name to. Our felt relationship with him feels flat and one dimensional because we are trying to pretend that our ultrasound pictures of him are actually him.

As a result of this misunderstanding, we approach the Bible not as the living and active word of God, but more like a photo album full of static pictures from some bygone era. We approach prayer to God not as a two-way conversation but more like leaving a recorded voice message on some divine answering machine because God for some reason never seems to take our calls.

We were not created for simply an awareness of God. We were made for *relationship* with him. We were not meant to have relationships with images. We were created to experience and be experienced by real, living things.

This has been God's definition of relationship since the beginning of time. In the Middle Ages, people experienced the *effects* of God without actually *experiencing* him. Today, we emphasize *awareness* of God without regard for *encountering* him.

That falls so short of God's intentions for you. That's a cheap, hollow definition of what relationship is. We'd be crazy to approach any other human relationship like that, so why do we do it with Jesus, the great lover of our souls?

For some of us, the concept of feeling God's presence can raise suspicions. Emotions are powerful and easily manipulated—often to the detriment of vulnerable people. The felt relationship I'm emphasizing here is not merely energetic hype or a light, airy sense of peace. While those feelings can certainly be part of communing with Jesus, they aren't the only experiences he invites us into. Following Jesus brings a wide spectrum of emotions, and they're not all positive or equally intense—much like the relationships you have with other people.

Some might cynically suggest that book knowledge is all we can have about God. But only one opinion matters, and that's Jesus'. He has so much more of himself for you to experience. God has so much more to show you, so much more for you to know.

Put down the pictures of Jesus. For a moment, leave behind the data, the measurements, the analysis. Clear the table and set a couple plates. Sweep the floors, open the blinds, start the oven. Open your ears, put your hand on the door, and hear the words of Jesus for you today:

> *Look! I stand at the door and knock. If you hear my voice and open the door, I will come in, and we will share a meal together as friends.* (Revelation 3:20)

Because for all this talk about the history of us knowing Jesus, we are missing a glaring reality:

He's already at your door,

and he wants to know *you,* too.

CHAPTER 2

YADA (PART 1)

My DAD AND I were parked in front of a strip mall in Maple Grove, Minnesota inside a 1995 Ford Taurus—dark green with a beige interior. The mid-summer sun was flowing freely through the un-tinted windows, and I was severely hot and mildly annoyed. It was the glorious mid-nineties, and I had much better things to do as an eight(ish)-year-old boy than to be my dad's sidekick on this asinine suburban strip-mall shopping trip.

Even as I wallowed in my self-loathing, I still loved my dad. Growing up, he was present, involved, and hard-working. He took care of my mom and our family well. I remember especially when he decided to make "snack supper." On some nights when my parents were too worn out to cook dinner, my dad would create a spread of crackers, cheese, meat, and cucumbers. So good. He was (and is!) a great dad.

But like all parents, my dad carried an aura of mystery around him. I knew about him as my *dad*, but what about the things that made him a *person, a man*? There's much more to a human than what they do on the surface or in just in front of us. There is a sacred "hiddenness" in all of us, something beautiful and deep. I wanted to know that part of my dad.

So for my father, I still had questions around who he was at his core. What were his fears? What were his greatest joys? What did he love about mom the most? How was marriage and family life hard for him? How did he feel about God? Who were his closest friends? What were the driving goals of his life? What made up his "hiddenness" that drove him to do what he did? I loved my dad, so I desired something greater than facts about him. I desired to encounter his personhood.

So back to me in the Ford Taurus. There I was, sweaty and still a little sour about being taken against my will on this stupid shopping trip. My dad invited me to come into the store with him, and I declined with slight sarcastic disgust. He walked into the store and left me alone in the passenger seat.

As the minutes ticked by, I started to get restless. What was taking him so long? When could I get back to my Nintendo? What was for dinner? So I started to explore around the car. I looked in the container in between the seats and found some gum wrappers, crumbs, a pen. Next up was the glove box. A Rand McNally atlas of the United States from five years ago, an insurance card, and the car owner's manual. That was interesting at least. I slammed the glove box door shut. Where was he?

In an attempt to ease my boredom, I searched around in the passenger door compartment. With my right hand, I felt around in the blind for something, anything interesting. My fingers came across something smooth and rectangular. It was a cassette tape. My dad only listened to the radio in the car, so this tape caught my attention. On the front was a picture of a man playing guitar with a spotlight shining on him. Bold orange lettering stood out next to the man, spelling out *Rattle and Hum*. Kinda cool I guess. In the top right I noticed more lettering, this time white and spelling out something I couldn't quite understand:

U2.

As I sat there, slightly confused and slightly interested, I noticed my dad walking back to the car. I was going to put the tape back where I found it, but something gripped me in that moment. I felt that I might have unearthed some deeper information about my father, kind of like Indiana Jones finding the Lost Ark. Music is such a powerful and personal thing, and here was a tape that Dad owned. *My dad.* I needed to listen to that tape. I wanted to discover something hidden about him.

He approached the driver's side door. I slid the tape into my pocket.

When we got home, I ran into my room and closed the door. I was the proud owner of a pretty sweet boombox from Target. (Remember, I'm from Minnesota. We get everything from Target up here.) Up until this point, my boombox had only played Mom-approved Christian music (I was a *huge* Amy Grant fan), but now my innocent speakers were about to get acquainted with something much different. I loaded the tape and pressed play, the volume low enough for just me to hear.

I pressed my ear against the speaker as the soft static stoked my anticipation. I heard the noise of a crowd then Bono's voice coolly and defiantly bellowed:

"This is a song Charles Manson stole from the Beatles, and we're stealing it back."

Whoa. I'm not even sure what that means.

Then The Edge's signature guitar sound cut through the static like a hot knife through butter. Bono started singing, the band continued to build like a summer afternoon thunderstorm behind him, and then it all broke loose.

Helter Skelter. Goodbye, Amy Grant. I'm a rocker now.

But you know what? More exciting than discovering the sound of U2 was discovering something else, something much more real:

My dad is a rocker. We are rockers together.

Who knew? My clean-cut, lawn mowing, Ford Taurus-driving, data analyst dad listened to rock and roll. I felt proud to be his son. Discovering this new treasure in my dad made me feel that way.

That day, I felt close to my dad on a deeper level. I found out something about him that seemed sacred and personal—something that made him *him*. I moved slightly away from knowing *about* my dad, and more toward *knowing him* as a man, as a real person. I encountered him in a way I never had before.

This is the goal for all true relationships—*to experience and be experienced by one another.*

Listen to Paul write on this in Galatians 4:8-9 (CSB):

> *But in the past, since you didn't know God, you were enslaved to things that by nature are not gods. But now, since you know God, or rather have become known by God, how can you turn back again to the weak and worthless elements? Do you want to be enslaved to them all over again?*

The point of Paul writing this was to call out the church for going back to their old ways of living, but do you see Paul's small clarification here? The Galatians have come to know God *and* God has come to know them. It goes both ways. He's defining true relationship with God.

Knowing and being known. This is the definition we will use for true relationship with God.

But don't take my word for it.

My highest form of theological education was Sunday School. Over the next few pages, we will look to the scriptures together and discover how the Bible itself calls us to be in true relationship with God. This chapter focuses on the first half of our definition above, *us knowing God*. Next chapter, we'll focus on the other half, *God knowing us*.

God's highest desire for us is to know him. He wants this for us more than anything. As a response, our highest desire should be to know him as well. Life has a crazy way of distracting us from that goal though. We are pulled in a million different ways from our ultimate need, knowing our creator.

In the book of Jeremiah, we see how anything, even good things from God, can distract us from God's ultimate desire and our ultimate need, truly knowing him.

Jeremiah was a major character in the Old Testament. He was a prophet, which meant that he was called to hear God speak to him and then speak to the people on his behalf. Jeremiah's words were literally the words of God, and the people were to take notice.

Jeremiah had the lovely task of rebuking God's people in Judah after they had disobeyed him. They'd made a covenant (a binding promise) to follow his rules and way of life, but they did not respect that covenant at all. Now it was Jeremiah's responsibility to deliver the consequences for their actions.

By Chapter 9 of Jeremiah, there has been warning after warning after warning. Jeremiah then takes a break from his regularly scheduled programming and writes this in verses 23-24:

> *This is what the Lord says:*
> *"Don't let the wise boast in their wisdom,*
> *or the powerful boast in their power,*
> *or the rich boast in their riches.*
>
> *But those who wish to boast should boast in this alone:*
> *that they truly know me and understand that I am*
> *the Lord*
> *who demonstrates unfailing love*
> *and who brings justice and righteousness to the earth,*
> *and that I delight in these things.*
>
> *I, the Lord, have spoken!"*

One could argue that the baseline problem with God's people was that they were prideful. And they kind of had a reason, right? Of all the people on the earth, God chose *them* to be his people. God busted them out of Egypt, cared for them as they wandered back to their homeland, cleared out the enemy nations that were living there, and established them in some of the most valuable real estate in all the world.

The thing is, in classic God fashion, he warned his people specifically about this back in Deuteronomy 8:10-18. God's plan was to provide abundantly for his people as they chose to hold up their end of the covenant promise with him. They would increase in population, land, and livestock because of God's blessing. As it is with us today, abundance tends to lead to distraction. We comfortably sink into lives of comfort and ease and forget the giver of our abundance, God himself. The nation of Judah was no exception. Once they got comfortable with the gifts God gave them, they neglected their worship to him and ended up taking credit for all their success and prosperity.

God's people had messed up, and their relationship was harmed. In an attempt to repair relationship with God, we humans tend to "make it up" to him in a couple of different ways:

Sometimes when we're caught in a sin, we turn to self-loathing and shame.

Sometimes, we indulge in legalism and rules to overcorrect.

Sometimes, we even receive consequences for our actions—a metaphorical return to Egypt.

But in this situation with Judah, God isn't primarily concerned with teaching his people a lesson. He doesn't want self-loathing, he isn't going to reveal an additional set of burdensome rules to live by, nor is he going to send them back into captivity for a time out. In verse 24, we see what God really desires:

> *"that they truly know me and understand that I am the Lord."*

To *truly* know and understand. That was God's dream for his people in Judah. It's his dream for you right now.

So underneath all that pride, all that sin, all that waywardness, was a faulty knowledge of God. There was no relationship. There was no experiencing him as Father God who freed them from slavery and brought them into freedom. When you don't regularly experience a relationship with someone, it's easy to lose sight of why you're in relationship to begin with. It's easy to drift away, to slowly lose consciousness, to fall asleep.

We all have those people in our lives whom we see only a few times per year. The smiley small talk and surface-level discussion about the weather and jobs is all an attempt to "catch up" while looking at the clock waiting for this awkward encounter to be over.

But it's awkward because we don't experience them consistently enough to call it a relationship. You don't miss them when you leave, and you aren't affected by their lack of presence. This was God and his people back in 600 BC.

Are you affected by God's lack of presence in your life?

Even more so, *does your answer bother you?*

What's interesting to me here is that there are *two* things God wants his people to boast in: that they *know* him, and that they *understand* him. Let's look a bit deeper. I'm no Hebrew expert, but I do have an iPhone with a Bible app on it. Here's what I found:

The Hebrew word for *understand* in this passage of Jeremiah is *haskel,* which is from the verb *sakal* (pronounced "saw-kal") which means to consider, be prudent, have insight, comprehend, or give attention to. The specific word *haskel* is only used two other times in Scripture, both in terms of wise intellectual understanding.

Keep that in mind as we focus on God's command to boast in *knowing him.* The Hebrew word for *know* used here is *weyadoa,* which is a derivative from the verb *yada* (pronounced "yaw-dah"). The most common definition of yada is "to know," and it can be used for a wide variety of knowing, from purely intellectual to strictly experiential, or a mixture of both. But due to the cultural climate we operate in that emphasizes rational thought over experience, *yada* is often overemphasized with regards to intellectual understanding and underemphasized in terms of knowledge through experience.

This book is an attempt to rebalance the definition of *yada* for the modern day. We need to recover the experiential side to knowing Jesus not at the expense of factual understanding, but in harmony with it.

The people of Jeremiah's time lived in the *enchanted* world we talked about. The kind of world where spirituality was as commonly experienced as the air breathed. So if you heard

Jeremiah instruct you to boast in knowing God, you wouldn't have retreated into your bedroom with the Torah to analyze it. You would have gone to the temple to hear, smell, see, *feel*. Knowing God was to experience him. *Yada* is so much more than just head knowledge.

In the Jeremiah 9 verse above, *sakal* and *yada* are included together. If God's intention was just for people to intellectually know of him, either *sakal or yada* would have been used. Either word can be used, on its own, to indicate that type of knowledge. *Sakal* usually means to know though wise understanding; *yada* usually means to know through experience. Our culture tends to boast in the first definition, but Jeremiah wants us to pursue both.

When I was in training to be a pilot, I needed to study aerodynamics—how planes fly. Early on in training, I studied the principles and concepts of flying while in a classroom on the ground. I went over how an airplane climbs, descends, turns, etc. At this point, my knowledge of flying was more in line with *sakal*.

How many of you would jump in a plane with me if I only knew about flying in terms of mental understanding like *sakal*? Don't worry, more training is involved.

I was eventually given the opportunity to fly the airplane all by myself. I was in charge of making it climb, turn, and descend. I used my knowledge from the classroom to help me actually move that Cessna 172 around in the sky. No longer did I learn about flying from a book; I learned by *experience*. I encountered flying by actually doing it. I learned how much force it took to turn, how slow to fly just before landing, and how to account for changing wind conditions. I gained knowledge by experience, which is what *yada* emphasizes.

And *yada* is what we are after in our relationship with God. *Yada* is used more than nine hundred times in the Bible. It means *to know* but when used to describe knowing God, it's a balanced meaning between intellect and experience.

The Bible is full of people gaining knowledge of God by experiencing him. The Old Testament especially contains some pretty vivid descriptions of God making himself tangibly felt. Sometimes God makes himself known to people who aren't even looking for him, like with Pharaoh in the story of the Exodus.

The story of the Exodus begins with God's people enslaved in Egypt under the harsh rule of Pharaoh, Egypt's god-like ruler. God calls up a man named Moses to lead his people out of Pharaoh's stubborn grip. Early on in the story we see Moses confront Pharaoh for the very first time and this is what he said as recorded in Exodus 5:1-2 (bracketed word added):

> *After this presentation to Israel's leaders, Moses and Aaron went and spoke to Pharaoh. They told him, "This is what the Lord, the God of Israel, says: Let my people go so they may hold a festival in my honor in the wilderness."*
>
> *"Is that so?" retorted Pharaoh. "And who is the Lord? Why should I listen to him and let Israel go? I don't know [yada] the Lord, and I will not let Israel go."*

Pharaoh turned down Moses' request to free God's people

because he *didn't know the God of his Hebrew slaves.* In the multi-god world of ancient Egypt, the Hebrew god was a non-factor. Pharaoh knew that the Hebrews worshiped *a god,* but he had no *experience* of *their God.* Like many of us today, Pharaoh's knowledge of God was unbalanced in favor of intellect.

Pharaoh was lacking experiential knowledge of YHWH, so God decided to fix that.

Ten plagues were unleashed on Egypt, each bringing its own form of power and terror to the Hebrews' slave masters. From the Nile river turning into blood, to thick swarms of flies blocking out the sun, to the death of all Egypt's livestock, finally ending with the silent death in the middle of the night of every firstborn Egyptian boy.

Now, Pharaoh *knew* the LORD.

Over the course of the ten plagues on Egypt, *yada* is used multiple times as the result of God *making himself known* through the plagues. Take these examples:

> *"When I raise my powerful hand and bring out the Israelites, the Egyptians will know* [yada] *that I am the Lord."* (Exodus 7:5, bracketed word added)
>
> *"But this time I will spare the region of Goshen, where my people live. No flies will be found there. Then you will know* [yada] *that I am the Lord and that I am present even in the heart of your land."* (Exodus 8:22, bracketed word added)

"If you don't, I will send more plagues on you and your officials and your people. Then you will know [yada] that there is no one like me in all the earth." (Exodus 9:14, bracketed word added)

See the pattern? The plagues were meant to make all of Egypt *know* God by *experiencing* his power. God was not just hoping for Pharaoh to understand on paper where he was coming from. He wanted Pharaoh to *feel* his majesty, the weight of his glory, his infinite power. And by *encountering* God, he would.

Jeremiah 16:21 (bracketed word added) paints a similar picture:

The Lord says,
"Now I will show them my power;
now I will show them my might.
At last they will know [yada] and understand
that I am the Lord."

God shows up, and the people *know him by experiencing* his power and might. How about this beautiful passage from Hosea 2:19-20 (bracketed word added):

I will make you my wife forever,
showing you righteousness and justice,
unfailing love and compassion.
I will be faithful to you and make you mine,
and you will finally know [yada] me as the Lord.

Look at all of God's actions here: God intends to be companions with us, showing us what it means to do right and hate what is wrong, to have compassion and love for others, and to see his faithfulness. God is doing all these things so that his people will finally know him.

In Jeremiah 9, God wants his people to take pride in the fact that they *understand God intellectually and know him by experience.* Because if God's people actually *experienced* him regularly, we'd have a whole different Old Testament story.

And I'm willing to bet that if you *experienced* God regularly, your life would look a whole lot different as well.

The narrative, poetic, and prophetic writings of the Old Testament all seem to land more on the experiential side of things. The first thirty-nine books of the Bible seem to emphasize a God who is regularly encountered both physically and spiritually. Things take a slight turn when we flip the page from Malachi to Matthew, in the New Testament.

In the Septuagint, which is the Greek translation of the Old Testament, we see the Hebrew word *yada* translated into the Greek word *ginosko* over 490 times. *Ginosko* is the primary Greek translation of *yada.*

Ginosko carries the same meaning as *yada* with regards to knowledge by perception or experience but there is a slight change in emphasis. In the New Testament, the writers appear to add the emphasis of *obedience in action* to the definition of truly knowing God. This might feel incongruent initially, but the New Testament's focus on action builds upon the experience of the Old Testament.

We all act based on experience. When you're thirsty, you drink water. When you're tired, you take a nap or grab a latte. When Gary Anderson misses the game winning field goal at the end of the 1998 NFC Championship football game, you run outside to cry in your snow fort by yourself, wondering why God chose you to be a Minnesota Vikings fan.

So in a way, the New Testament's emphasis on *action* in addition to *experience* is not meant to totally kick experiencing God to the curb. Rather, *ginosko* builds on what *yada* started. The New Testament adds to the narrative arc of what it means to know God by balancing feeling with action. This prevents us from simply desiring an "experience" of God and calling it good. What matters is what you do with that experience. If you truly experienced God and believed in his relentless love for you, actions will follow. If the Israelites truly experienced God, their actions would have been different, and Jeremiah would have been out of a job. Actions are born out of experience; they don't replace it. I am on a very slim house church pastor budget so forgive me for the incredibly basic design of the following diagram:

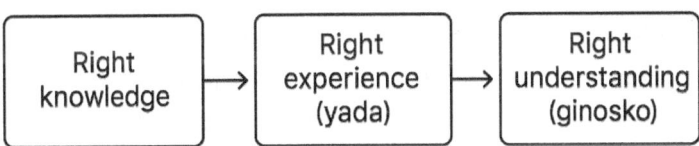

If we remove any one element from the diagram above, we lose the full meaning of knowing God as the whole library of Scripture describes. If we remove intellectual knowledge (understanding), we won't be able to evaluate our experiences of God to see if they're in line with God's intentions or not. If we remove experiencing him, we turn into emotionless robots that relate to God more like an employer than a Father. If we remove action, our relationship to God turns into a mushy, self-centered faith that values feeling over obedience.

In my observation, the western church tends to remove the middle element from that poorly designed diagram I just created. This removal of experiencing God has major impacts on our obedience to him, which is what most churches are rightly trying to encourage. Remember, humans tend to act based on experience. So when we remove experience, our actions feel constructed, artificial, and forced. Jesus doesn't desire robotic obedience, he wants *a heart that wants to obey*, and this purity of heart is created in the refining fires of an experienced relationship. We learn how to be in relationship with someone through experiencing them.

For example, my wife likes a clean, organized house. That's her general desire. So most of the time, I work to make sure the places I left are in orderly condition because I know that she appreciates that.

But during the school year from the hours of four p.m. to eight p.m., our house is in chaos. The kids are running around, stressed out about homework, processing the highs and lows from the day, and needing to be fed and put to bed.

If I were to spend that time cleaning the upstairs bathroom by myself while my wife was left with our incredibly emotional children, I would not be doing right by my wife. This is like jumping straight from intellectual understanding to action.

Our relationship is mature enough for me to know that even though she has a desire for a clean house, sometimes she has a different will. I only know her will in the moment by knowing her personally. I've made enough errors in judgment to learn that after school, I need to be present with the kids and not doing my own thing. It's through experiencing my wife over a long period of time that I have learned to love her through my actions.

Just think about pastors who sacrifice their families in favor of doing "God's work." They spend every waking moment devoted to their church ministry while neglecting their first ministry, their families. Doesn't God want us to devote our entire lives to him? Yes, but not at the expense of those you love. That's an immature way of looking at things. They would have realized that if they *experienced* Jesus instead of just *knew about* what he said.

In Matthew 7:21-23, a bunch of people looked like they were doing the will of God, but they were missing the point entirely. They were casting out raging demons and performing incredible miracles, all in the name of Jesus. Instead of praising and affirming them, Jesus tells them to politely get out of his face and go away. Even though they acted in the name of Jesus, they *weren't known by him.* It's kind of like walking into the kitchen of a random stranger and starting to demo the cabinets because you decided to gift them a kitchen makeover. The owner of the house would be standing there, shellshocked at the holes in the drywall while they quickly dialed 911.

Actions don't matter unless there's relationship, and relationships are *experienced.*

The emphasis of *ginosko* in the New Testament is on the actions that follow experience. Take a look at some of these other passages to illustrate what I mean:

> *I want to know* [ginosko] *Christ and experience the mighty power that raised him from the dead. I want to suffer with him, sharing in his death.* (Philippians 3:10, bracketed word added)

Paul desired to know Jesus through experience *and* action. He wants to encounter the power that raised Jesus from the dead while also desiring to suffer as Jesus did. Paul's *action* here is suffering because in Paul's mind, to suffer for Jesus is to know him. And living in him, suffering for him, also produces a more Spirit-led lifestyle:

> *Anyone who continues to live in him will not sin. But anyone who keeps on sinning does not know* [ginosko] *him or understand who he is.* (1 John 3:6, bracketed word added)

First John 3:6 is as clear as day: A follower of Jesus who claims to know Jesus yet shows no movement toward holy living does not actually know him. Those who truly know Jesus develop the *action* of fighting their sinful nature.

To experience Jesus and to live a life in response to that experience is the fullest definition of knowing God. Our regular encountering of Christ leads us to live our lives in obedient response. And as we dive deeper into obedience, we find still more depth of relationship. Experience is the catalyst for action, and action is the driver of greater experience. We need to enter into this beautiful rhythm of relationship to spiritually survive, but this is easier said than done. God, in his desire for us, will often use experiences that we would never choose to wake us up to the reality that there's so much more of him to encounter.

My wife and I were at the twenty-week ultrasound for our first child, a normally joyful occasion. I can still remember how that exam room looked. The cold tile floor. The lights dimmed to help watch the ultrasound screen. The low hum of the ventilation fan.

After our ultrasound, we waited around for about twenty minutes before a doctor came in. It was the way she said those words that still haunts me today.

"We aren't seeing what we need to see on your daughter's ultrasound."

She said those words, exactly.

My body froze up. I remember myself tearfully convulsing, breathing in that stale, recycled air. Our lives changed in an instant. They told us they weren't sure if our daughter would make it. If she did, her life would be radically different. We drove home, weeping. I was so sad, confused, lost. But you know what I felt most of all?

Anger.

I had devoted my entire life thus far to being a good Christian man. I was actively involved at church as a worship leader, went on a few mission trips, and was a kind enough guy to warrant Jesus' love. Is this the thanks I get, God? What are you doing here? Why are you doing this to me?

I let it all go. I looked God in the face and screamed in rage at him.

He looked back at me and said nothing.

Now, eleven years removed from that day, things are so much different between God and me. That day in the exam room opened the door to an *experience* of God. Suffering has a way of doing that, doesn't it? The pathway through the dense forest of faith is often cleared by trial and pain.

When I look back on that day, in all its sadness and pain, and reflect on the raw, angry, tearful questions I asked that day, I now know the answer. God weaved this painful thing into my life for one purpose:

That I would know him.

Not only did I *experience him,* but I've *acted* on that experience. My wife and I traded our dream of a safe, comfortable neighborhood for living in a part of our city with deep beauty mingled with deep tragedy and pain. We exchanged the dream of a simple, quiet biological family for a family whose purpose is to include people outside of our biological circle. We bought a house and put a big table in it.

We all have stories like this. Our lives were supposed to go a certain way, but they took a dark turn to a place we didn't want to go. These undesirable detours brought pain, resistance, confusion, and conflict. I hope that out of those detours, you're able to see the hope God could have been planting, the relationship you might have been cultivating, because of that darkness.

When life goes dark, it's only natural to wonder where we went wrong. We want order out of the chaos, a glimmer of light in the dark night, some information to make sense of our recently upended lives. But what if God wasn't trying to teach you some lesson or get you to know some facts about him that you previously were unaware of. What if, through real and deep pain, God's purpose was to *bring you to himself*?

Or in the words of Jesus in John 9, it could have happened so the power of God could be seen in you. And by *experiencing* God's power, you'd move to *act* in ways you never thought possible.

So at the end of your life you wouldn't boast in

Your house

Your car

Your family

Your job

Your wealth

Your influence

Your realized dreams

Your power

Your beauty

Your health

Your image

Your self

But rather, like with Jeremiah, you would boast in one thing only:

That you knew God.

The Bible presents a unified message on what it means to know God. We know God by experiencing him and then acting on that experience. But this is only half of our full definition of being in true relationship with God. The other half, *being known by God*, is equally important but incredibly underemphasized in our churches today.

CHAPTER 3

YADA (PART 2)

I was done.

Done with parenting. Done with being a husband. I was going to retire from caring for anyone else ever again. I had a good run, but the time had come to hang it up.

My wife and I felt called to help raise kids from hard places. Through the example and encouragement from other followers of Jesus, we expanded our idea of family to include children from unhealthy families in need of care. We were in the trenches. We had little kids of our own while answering this burning desire to love other children in our city. They needed a safe place to call home for however long. But the old adage is true: Hurting people hurt people, and I was being hurt by the people I was trying to help.

I had bitten off more than I could chew, and the demands of being a husband and father exceeded my mental and emotional capacity. I remember being confused, questioning Jesus about why I felt so stressed out when I was supposedly doing his will.

Doesn't God supply all my needs according to the riches found in Jesus? Isn't the burden of Jesus easy and light? Why is my life getting harder the more I try to obey?

My experience was not lining up with what I read in the Bible. If this was the life of faith, I wasn't sure I wanted it.

On that particularly hard day, I made a call to my friend Eric—someone in my life I look up to. A lot of times, I try to imitate Eric as he follows Jesus. Eric and his family are also one of the main reasons my wife and I continue to choose sacrifice over comfort, risk over safety, the hard road of faithfulness over the false comfort of self-centeredness. So in a way, this was his fault, and I was gonna vent to him.

I picked up the phone and told him about everything. The lying, the disrespect, the running away, the constant stress. The feeling that I've thrown away my life for nothing. I must have vented for five straight minutes to him, letting the expletives fly. He said nothing in return.

Once I got the big stuff off my chest, I expected him to help me talk through everything over the phone. I expected him to run through the theological principles of why we should endure in serving and loving our families, how Jesus loves us, how he calls us to pick up our cross daily, all that Christianese lingo. But strangely enough, he didn't say any of that. After a short pause, in a calm, compassionate voice, he said,

"Matt, do you want to come over?"

After debating a short while, I agreed. I'd be able to get out of my house for a bit at least. I drove the six or so blocks to his house, and I found Eric sitting on his front steps. In his hand he had an orange, square package.

It was a Reese's Peanut Butter Cup.

I walked up the steps, and he handed it to me and told me to eat it. He asked me to tell him everything that was on my heart again, minus the expletives because his kids were around. So between bites, I processed out loud my fears, anger, frustrations, and doubts. In classic Eric fashion, he just sat there as I talked. After a while he put his hand on my back and told me he loved me.

That was it.

Eric didn't try to fix me. He didn't logically reason with me. He didn't even pull out any Bible verses to share. He just listened. And through his listening, through the quiet of his presence just sitting with me, I felt something rare, something beautiful and deep.

I felt known.

Eric experienced my inner world; he saw the real me. He felt my raw emotion and he didn't run away. I felt something that no theologically correct sermon, well-written article, or thought-provoking podcast was ever able to make me feel. I knew the truths of the Bible that applied to the situation. I was able to point to different theological concepts that addressed my fears around sacrificing or Jesus. All those truths were well rehearsed.

I knew the truth, but I didn't believe it in that moment. Perhaps you can relate.

As Christians, we usually know the verses. We know the songs. But it's still a struggle to believe what we're reading and singing. I feel like I can physically hear the father of the demon-possessed child in Matthew 9 when he cries out, "I do believe, but help me overcome my unbelief!"

Through my experience of being known, I felt the peace of Jesus swell up in my heart again. I cried for a bit, then, full of the presence of the Holy Spirit, I drove back home. I was reenergized, recentered, and ready to continue my obedience to Jesus.

Eric demonstrated our *real relationship*. The kind where we experience someone else as well as allow them to experience us. God has designed us to know him *and to be known by him.*

For many of us, being known by God has taken a back seat to knowing him for ourselves. The default (yet incomplete) assumption in many of our churches today is that we experience God by knowing more things about him. So why not emphasize knowing more about him? Why not devote all our time, energy, resources, sermons, podcasts, small groups, Sunday school classes, and youth group events around knowing more stuff about God? Isn't that the way to relationship with him?

Again, this emphasis is not wrong, it's just incomplete and unbalanced.

That approach to knowing God is something that Descartes would affirm, not Jesus. You are not just a *Res Cogitan;* you are a dynamic, thinking, *and* feeling child of God, made in his image.

The Bible has no shortage of instances where *God experiences us.* In these places, we see a highly personal God who sees and hears us in whatever state we are. He even appears to be *affected* by our circumstances.

Early on in God's big story of pursuing his people back into relationship with him, we meet the first major character in God's plan, Abram. In Genesis 12, God tells Abram that through him and his offspring, God will accomplish his plan for reunification. This is great and all, but Abram and his wife Sarai are old—I mean *really old*. Having babies was out of the question. But Abram trusts God and waits for his promised offspring to arrive.

He waits. And waits. And then waits some more. Ten years go by and still Abram and Sarai do not have a child. So, the obvious impatience and distrust set in, and Sarai comes up with a plan to solve all this: Abram would sleep with Sarai's Egyptian slave Hagar who would conceive the child God promised. What could go wrong?

A lot, apparently.

Hagar ends up conceiving, but Sarai feels jealous at her ability to so quickly have a child. In her jealousy, Sarai starts to mistreat Hagar severely, so much so that Hagar, pregnant with child, runs into the desert to escape.

Hagar was caught in the middle of a poorly executed plan to wrestle control from God. She was sexually used and a victim of abuse. Alone in the harsh, unforgiving desert, her pregnant belly reminded her that she was in real danger with no one to turn to, nowhere to run.

That is until an angel from God confronts her by a desert spring. Here's the narrative from Genesis 16:7-14:

> *The angel of the Lord found Hagar beside a spring of water in the wilderness, along the road to Shur. The angel said to her, "Hagar, Sarai's servant, where have you come from, and where are you going?"*
>
> *"I'm running away from my mistress, Sarai," she replied.*
>
> *The angel of the Lord said to her, "Return to your mistress, and submit to her authority." Then he added, "I will give you more descendants than you can count."*
>
> *And the angel also said, "You are now pregnant and will give birth to a son. You are to name him Ishmael (which means 'God hears'), for the Lord has heard your cry of distress. This son of yours will be a wild man, as untamed as a wild donkey! He will raise his fist against everyone, and everyone will be against him. Yes, he will live in open hostility against all his relatives."*
>
> *Thereafter, Hagar used another name to refer to the Lord, who had spoken to her. She said, "You are the God who sees me." She also said, "Have I truly seen the One who sees me?" So that well was named Beer-lahai-roi (which means "well of the Living One who sees me"). It can still be found between Kadesh and Bered.*

The angel continues to explain that due to Sarai's attempt to control the situation, Hagar's child will not be the one God uses to bring about his plan of redemption. But notice the name of the child—*Ishmael,* which means *God hears.*

And because God heard her in the wilderness, Hagar decides to call God a new name, *the God who sees me.*

In Hebrew, this name is *El-Roi,* and the significance is staggering.

The one to make the first move here was God. He initiated the relationship by questioning and listening. The angel essentially asks *"Hagar, what are you doing here?"* A strange question for the ambassador of the all-knowing creator of the universe to ask, don't you think?

This is all a part of the process of God to *know Hagar.* Yes, it's true that God already knew the answer. He knew all about the situation with Hagar and Sarai. He knew about Sarai's mistrust, the abuse, and Hagar's flight into the desert.

But God wanted to hear it from her. This was an opportunity for Hagar to confess, to be vulnerable, to cry out in her misery.

Hagar was honest about her pain with God. As a result, he was able to know her differently than if he would have done all the initiating and responding himself. Remember, true relationship is *experiencing and being experienced,* or *knowing and being known.* Because Hagar was given the opportunity to cry out to God, she was given the opportunity *to be known.* This opened the door for a two-way relationship to take place, which prompted her to call God *El-Roi,* or the *God who sees.*

A God who sees us carries important implications for our relationship with him. For one, a God who *sees us* is very different from a God who is simply *aware of us.* A God who sees us is a God with whom connection is possible because he gives us the dignity of approaching him freely with our true selves.

I felt known on the porch with Eric because he gave me the opportunity to tell him, in my own words, how I was feeling. Eric could have started the conversation with "*I know how hard it's been. You've told me. Keep trusting Jesus.*" While true, that would have landed completely different with me, and I would have walked away without feeling known. Eric only knew what was going on in a factual, black-and-white kind of way. Sharing with him is what makes my situation *known* to him, what makes me *known* by him.

I worry *we have settled for a God who is simply aware of us.* He sees us, for sure. But to be *known* by him is so much more.

God sees you right now. This sight is not simply a stale, cold awareness but a deep, intimate acquaintance with *all of you.* Go ahead and read Psalm 139 sometime and discover just how deep his knowledge of you is. God leaves no stone unturned, not one part of the landscape of your heart is foreign territory to him. Joys and pain, fears and dreams, hidden or not, he feels it all.

And here is where it gets amazing: *He wants you to tell him all about those things right now.* He wants you to bring your whole self to him *not so that you can inform him about the things he already knows about you,* but so that *you can have the opportunity to be seen and known by him,* and by being seen, experience the kind of relationship he desires with you.

God's ability to reorganize and respond to the sounds coming from his creation is arguably one of his most beautiful traits. God *hears his people.* The simple act of hearing was the catalyst for one of the most important events in the history of the world: the Exodus.

God's people found themselves in Egypt due to a horrible famine that ravaged the surrounding area. Seeking relief, the Israelites took themselves to Egypt, one of the most powerful empires at the time. At first, life was great for the Israelites in Egypt. They had a well-liked representative high up in the Egyptian government (Joseph), access to food during a severe famine, and the security of living in one of the most powerful empires of that time.

So what do you do if you're feeling secure and hopeful about the future? You have babies. Lots of babies.

The Israelite population in Egypt expanded so rapidly and with such force that the Egyptian government took notice. By this time Joseph was long gone, and a new ruler in Egypt had risen to power. The person of Joseph had been forgotten among the Egyptian government, and the new Pharaoh was looking at the ever-increasing population of Israelites in Egypt with an uneasy feeling in his chest. He was afraid the Israelites were becoming too numerous, too powerful, and could eventually pose a threat to his native Egyptians.

So Pharaoh enslaved every Israelite in Egypt. Utilizing incredible amounts of punishment, hard labor, and violence, the Egyptians hoped to wear the Israelites out and stop their growth.

Whole cities were built on the bloody backs of Israelite men. Pharaoh also ordered every baby Israelite boy to be murdered as soon as they were born. Because the Israelite women gave birth before the executioners could get to them, Pharaoh then decreed that every newborn Israelite baby boy would be thrown into the raging Nile River as soon as possible after birth.

Can you imagine the *sounds*?

The quivering groaning of the Israelite men taking another load of building materials as the whips snapped on their backs?

The violent wailing of new mothers as their baby boys were wrestled away from them soon after birth?

The fragile, gurgling cries of infants as they drowned in the Nile?

It's haunting. And God had enough. We read this in Exodus 2:23-25 (CSB):

> *After a long time, the king of Egypt died. The Israelites groaned because of their difficult labor, they cried out, and their cry for help because of the difficult labor ascended to God. God heard their groaning, and God remembered his covenant with Abraham, with Isaac, and with Jacob. God saw the Israelites, and God knew.*

Under the incredible violence of the Egyptians, the Israelites cried out to God. And make no mistake, their prayers weren't lost in the universe somewhere. They rose up to God and he heard them. And because God heard them, he remembered.

Here it is again: God *remembered*. We are in the same paradox we found ourselves in with Hagar when the angel asked her what she was up to out in the desert. The tension between an all-knowing supreme ruler of the universe and these little incidents of God "remembering" seem to be at odds.

If we take the whole library of Scripture, it points to a God who doesn't forget, who doesn't need reminding, and who isn't too busy to remember. Again, we can hold two things in tension here: that God is all-knowing *and* at least from our viewpoint on the earth, in our limited understanding and reasoning, *he can remember.*

The purpose of this tension in Scripture is not to give us some fun theological concept to argue about. Its purpose is to illustrate what we've been discovering all along: *God can experience us.*

God's act of remembering when he heard the cries of his people is meant to show you that he contains the ability to be affected by you. And this opens the door for genuine relationship with him.

If you think about it, this is the whole reason why we pray. We pray because we believe God hears us. We wouldn't pray if we thought God wasn't affected by our prayers. We speak, and he responds.

So God heard his people, and he remembered his promises to them…*and God knew.* It's one thing to hear someone. It's one thing to be reminded of something because of that hearing. But the fact that the Holy Spirit desired to show us that God *knew* as a result of all this is incredible.

The Hebrew word used in "God knew" is the same word we've been learning about together. Remember that one?

Yada. Knowing by experiencing. It was the *cries* of his children that moved God the Father to act.

Last week I was coaching my son's basketball practice, and I ran across a similar situation. I had the kids play a simulated game, with the promise of watermelon Gatorade for the victors. To a six-year-old boy, watermelon Gatorade is like liquid gold; they'll do anything to taste that sweet nectar. So the boys played hard—so hard that one of them caught an elbow to the eye while trying to grab a loose basketball.

At first he toughed it out. I could see him out of the corner of my eye as he winced and held his palm over his face. His face was like a kettle of water just about to boil, rumbling and quivering. After ten seconds of suppressed emotion, the pain became so bad that he let it all out. His face got red, his eyes slammed shut, and the tears started flowing. His hurt became a rolling boil in the center of a middle-school basketball court.

At that moment, I saw his father run onto the court, with our game still in progress, to hug his boy. His father had surely seen his son get that elbow to the face. He saw him try his best to continue on with his buddies, but once his son started to cry in the middle of that loud, busy gym, all bets were off. He moved from being *aware* of his child's hurt to *experiencing* it through his tears. His father knew his child through a combination of factual knowledge (he got hurt because of an elbow to the face) and personal experience (my son is crying in pain, so as his father, I will attend to him).

Just like the father and son on our basketball court, God experienced his people through their tears. To tearfully cry out is to let down all the walls, to let go of all the pretense. Noticing the tears of someone else does something *to us*. It's an encounter with truth laid bare that demands a response.

God experiences us.

God *yada*(s) you the same way you *yada* him. God knows you through a combination of factual knowledge and personal experience. Just like you know him.

In the story above, we see God *coming to an* awareness of something. There are also examples in Scripture where God experiences the emotion of someone and appears to change his mind regarding a future event. In 2 Kings 19-20, we meet King Hezekiah, who had just prayed for God to save his people from the Assyrians who were ready to attack. God listened and miraculously saved his people because of the prayer of Hezekiah. As the miracle was unfolding, Hezekiah became very sick, and he was visited by the prophet Isaiah who delivered the somber news that Hezekiah would eventually die due to his illness.

Hezekiah, fresh off witnessing the miracle God worked for his people, turns to face the wall of his palace and pleads with God. Many commentators suggest that Hezekiah's act of turning to the wall was an attempt to conceal his emotions from the people in the room. He was a king, and kings do not cry in public.

The tears were flowing, the suppressed groans were sneaking out, and God was listening. The scene switches back to Isaiah as he is leaving the palace. God has a new message for Isaiah to tell the King in 2 Kings 20:4-5:

> *But before Isaiah had left the middle courtyard, this message came to him from the Lord: "Go back to Hezekiah, the leader of my people. Tell him, 'This is what the Lord, the God of your ancestor David, says: I have*

heard your prayer and seen your tears. I will heal you, and three days from now you will get out of bed and go to the Temple of the Lord."

Isaiah tells Hezekiah that God has heard his prayer and has seen his tears. The Hebrew word used for "see" here is *raah* which, according to James Strong, means to see with perception or understanding. *Raah* means to not only view physically, but to gain understanding and insight from what you've just seen.

God saw the tears of the king and perceived what they meant. In other words, God experienced Hezekiah through his tears and changed his future intentions with his life.

The Bible shares of a God who experiences us. Because of this experience, God is seen to possess the ability to gain awareness (as with the Israelites in Egypt) and to shift his intentions (like with King Hezekiah). We need to balance these depictions with other pieces of Scripture that seem to indicate that God knows the future (Isaiah 46:10) and he will not be subject to any will other than his own (Psalm 115:3). All these descriptors of God are true.

I understand there's a lot of debate out there regarding whether or not God actually changed his mind. Did God have one plan, then after listening to Hezekiah, completely change his mind? I guess only God knows that. What we know, from our vantage point, is that is certainly looks like God changed his mind because of the experience of Hezekiah's sorrow.

This pleading with God was not just confined to normal, everyday people. Even Jesus himself is seen wondering if there was any way other than his death to accomplish the will of God.

Distressed in spirit, with his face in the dirt, we read Jesus' gut-wrenching cry to his Father in Matthew 26:39 (CSB):

> *Going a little farther, he fell facedown and prayed, "My Father, if it is possible, let this cup pass from me. Yet not as I will, but as you will."*

Here is Jesus (fully God) praying to the Father (also fully God) asking him to reconsider his death on the cross. Does anyone else find this a little confusing? He even asks the question a second time in verse 42. Twice, Jesus wonders aloud if anything else could be done to change his destiny.

Even Jesus was given the freedom to plead with the Father to change his mind. Was God ever going to change his mind? Nope. We understand through Scripture that the cross was always the plan. Jesus was always going to be sacrificed for our salvation. But the fact that Jesus still pleads with the Father is telling.

This exchange between the son and the Father was meant to illustrate the close bond Jesus had with his father. The kind of unity he prays that we would have in John 15. Jesus wasn't a robot soldier who prayed robotic prayers to a distant, unaffected robot commander. The loving relationship between the Father and the Son was so real. As Jesus was taking his final breaths, he even cried out to his father, choking on his own blood:

> *"My God, my God, why have you abandoned me?"*
> (Matthew 27:46b CSB)

The reformed part of me wants to say "C'mon Jesus, you knew

this was the plan all along. God predestined it. What's with the surprise?"

But that's not the point the Holy Spirit wanted to make when he inspired these words to be recorded. The point of Jesus' raw, desperate cry out to the Father was to illustrate the *yada* type of relationship he had with him. Jesus fully knew that this was the plan. But in that moment, the emotional intimacy he felt with his Father eclipsed all the rational thoughts about what needed to happen to obtain our chance at reunion with God. At that moment on the cross, the felt relationship between Jesus and his Father was the realest thing Jesus was feeling in that moment.

That feeling transcended his head knowledge. His heart cried out, and the Father *heard him.*

Now I hope you are starting to see the beautiful picture of what the Bible paints as real relationship with God. Not as one-sided as you might have thought, eh? *God experiences you in a way that maintains his complete authority yet invites you to interact with him as a dynamic, affected being.*

After all that seeing and hearing, after all God's *yada* of us, there's one more beautiful aspect of God's experiencing of us to consider: God remembers. He doesn't forget our sorrows. He doesn't "move on" like we do, hoping that the passage of time will erase the pains of the past. As we read in Psalm 56:8, God holds on to *everything*:

> *You keep track of all my sorrows. You have collected all my tears in your bottle. You have recorded each one in your book.*

Friend, as you read this book, I don't care if you learn anything. I don't care if I give you more knowledge, or more things to think on or ponder. My prayer for you is this: *that you would believe in a God who actually cares about you and is affected by your interactions with him.*

Isn't it crazy to think that with all God's "running the universe" responsibilities, that he has a bottle with every one of your tears in it?

The tears you shed when that dream died?

The tears that fell when the person you loved walked out on you?

The tears you cried when you grieved that incredible loss?

The tears of shame as you repented (again) from that sin you can't seem to escape?

Make no mistake. As a child of God, not one of your tears were shed apart from your heavenly Father knowing it fell. Not a single one.

As we have seen, the God of the Bible is a God who sees, hears, and knows you. He *is a God who experiences you.* And because he has the ability to experience you, a real, heartfelt relationship is possible. This is contrasted with the false relationship that the idols in our lives hold us with. An idol is anything in your life that distracts you from finding that deep relationship in God. These idols can be people, ideas, dreams, or anything we give ourselves to in the hopes of feeling purpose or meaning.

In Psalm 115, the Psalmist details how idols might look like they can experience us but actually can't. They have mouths but can't speak words of comfort to us. They have ears, but they will never be able to sit with us as we release the pent-up disappointment we are too afraid to show. They appear to have hands but will never wipe away the tears we shed in secret.

Idols can't experience us. Your dream of a perfect life doesn't care if you're hurting. Material possessions don't hear you if you're crying. A pristine body, beautiful house, or dream job won't move toward you in compassion when your face is pressed against your bedroom wall in grief.

When you're hurting, your idols will leave you alone and wait until you get over it.

Jesus moves toward your hurt. He isn't afraid to experience your pain. He'll go wherever he needs to go to get to you. Even into a tomb.

In Chapter 11 of the Gospel of John, we get to read the powerful story of the raising of Lazarus. He was a friend of Jesus, someone who Jesus really loved. At the beginning of the story, Jesus is told that Lazarus is very sick and about to die. We read Jesus' response in verses 4-11:

> But when Jesus heard about it he said, "Lazarus's sickness will not end in death. No, it happened for the glory of God so that the Son of God will receive glory from this." So although Jesus loved Martha, Mary, and Lazarus, he stayed where he was for the next two days. Finally, he said to his disciples, "Let's go back to Judea."
>
> But his disciples objected. "Rabbi," they said, "only a few days ago the people in Judea were trying to stone you. Are

you going there again?"

Jesus replied, "There are twelve hours of daylight every day. During the day people can walk safely. They can see because they have the light of this world. But at night there is danger of stumbling because they have no light." Then he said, "Our friend Lazarus has fallen asleep, but now I will go and wake him up."

After he heard Lazarus is gravely ill, Jesus confidently declares that this isn't the end for him. Jesus can say this because he is fully God. He has all the power that created the universe at his disposal. Raising someone from the dead is no big deal for him.

Many readers (including you) are probably pretty comfortable with Jesus' response so far. Of course he can raise Lazarus; he's God! All-powerful, miracle-working, death-defeating! Amen! But the story takes an interesting turn when Jesus actually visits (and gets to experience) the grave of Lazarus in verses 30-35:

Jesus had stayed outside the village, at the place where Martha met him. When the people who were at the house consoling Mary saw her leave so hastily, they assumed she was going to Lazarus's grave to weep. So they followed her there. When Mary arrived and saw Jesus, she fell at his feet and said, "Lord, if only you had been here, my brother would not have died."

When Jesus saw her weeping and saw the other people wailing with her, a deep anger welled up within him, and he was deeply troubled. "Where have you put him?" he asked them.

They told him, "Lord, come and see."

Then Jesus wept.

Confident Jesus then becomes highly emotional. Bold assurance gives way to anger and sorrow. He is deeply troubled. What happened to the strong, faith-filled Jesus from before?

He *saw* Mary weeping and he *heard* the wailing of the crowd.

Jesus goes from *knowing of* the sorrow Lazarus' death caused, to *experiencing* it.

In the story of Lazarus, we see a beautiful and compelling picture of the exact nature of God. Jesus' actions in this story are the exact representation of God's nature (Hebrews 1:3). Jesus isn't putting on a show, he isn't being over dramatic, and he isn't exaggerating to prove a point. *Jesus' response to Lazarus' death is God's real, authentic response.*

Jesus' confidence is true. God has the power to raise people from the dead. There is nothing too hard for him. Jesus is the sovereign ruler over everything, and nothing escapes his control, not even death. Jesus is sure Lazarus will rise because Jesus knows his own power.

Jesus' anger is true. The Greek words used here to describe Jesus' anger allude to a horse snorting as it gets ready to charge against an enemy. Sort of like a raging bull ready to fight. This is what Jesus feels as he enters into the pain of his friends as Lazarus lies dead. This isn't how it's supposed to be. Jesus' nostrils flare at the thought of death winning, even as Jesus fully knows how the story ends.

Jesus' sadness is also true. Here we see the king of the universe with tears falling down his face. The one who "upholds all things by the power of his word" struggles to speak under the weight of his own sadness. Again, Jesus knows Lazarus walks out of that tomb, yet he still feels profound sadness over how death comes over his beloved friend, even for a moment.

Jesus stood among the crowd mourning Lazarus and entered into their pain and sadness.

Over time, as we keep suppressing our truest feelings and hiding them from God, our hearts grow cold and hard. First to God, and also to other people. We become shells of our true selves, projecting a false joyfulness and strength while pushing the hard stuff down deeper and deeper into our hearts. Maybe that's you today. Underneath the happy face, the perky personality, the joyful exterior, lies an inner world full of anxiety, fear, sadness, and anger. Over time, perhaps you've gotten really good at cultivating this *public self* while dismissing and hiding your *private reality*.

We all want to be loved and accepted for who we are, but our fears of abandonment force us to put on a show for others in hopes they won't leave. Our true selves are too dangerous to let out. We're too broken, too mistake-prone, too fragile to expose our deepest selves. Who would want to willingly sit in my messy life with me? What kind of person would be able to love me even in my brokenness? Who on earth would voluntarily choose to experience me and my foul-smelling sinfulness?

I need to show you this from the ending of our Lazarus story. Read the following from John 11:39-44:

> *"Roll the stone aside," Jesus told them.*

But Martha, the dead man's sister, protested, "Lord, he has been dead for four days. The smell will be terrible."

Jesus responded, "Didn't I tell you that you would see God's glory if you believe?" So they rolled the stone aside. Then Jesus looked up to heaven and said, "Father, thank you for hearing me. You always hear me, but I said it out loud for the sake of all these people standing here, so that they will believe you sent me." Then Jesus shouted, "Lazarus, come out!" And the dead man came out, his hands and feet bound in graveclothes, his face wrapped in a headcloth. Jesus told them, "Unwrap him and let him go!"

Jesus was going to raise Lazarus from the dead, but Martha protested. Lazarus had been dead too long, his body was too decomposed, and the putrid stench would be too strong to even enter the tomb.

Jesus, with the tear stains on his cheeks still fresh, paid no attention to the protest of Martha. The stone door was rolled away, and the smell of death poured out from the opening of the tomb.

Then Jesus, with the same voice that hung the stars in the sky, called into the grave for his friend to come out.

And Lazarus walked out.

Do you hear the call of Jesus for you today? You've been hiding the dead parts of your heart for a long time. Your hidden self is reeking of anxiety, fear, and doubt. You might be protesting like Martha, insisting that your true self is too offensive to encounter.

Whatever skeletons you have hiding in your closet, Jesus isn't scared of them. He's not intimidated by your true, broken, beautiful, image-of-God self. He wants your whole being, with all its beautiful and ugly, miraculous and mundane, revealed and hidden.

God's dream for you is real, experienced relationship. We need to take steps on that journey. Maybe you're being honest with yourself right now and admitting you've never really experienced a true relationship with God. Or perhaps you once tasted the sweetness of intimately walking with Jesus only to find yourself today hungering for a return to that closeness.

Wherever you are today, there is a path forward, there is a way out of the dark tomb. There is a way to cultivate connection with the creator of the universe, right now, in your specific situation, with the life you're already living. There is a way to return to the harmonious *yada* relationship that Jesus desires for you.

If you have spent your life living on facts about Jesus, settling for awareness over experience, that has functioned as your own personal tomb. Facts create boxes—containers which are helpful for storing last night's meatloaf, but not for maintaining relationship with Jesus. Your walk with Christ is a living, breathing thing, meant not for the darkness and familiarity of only factual information, but for the midday sun of real, felt encountering.

So hear the call of Jesus today,

and come out.

CHAPTER 4

BRIDGES

AFTER (A) REALIZING we live in a "buffered" world that has since prioritized intellect over experience, and (b) relearning what it means to truly know (yada) and be known (also yada) by God, I hope you find yourself a little eager to break into new territory with God. Maybe some part of you senses the possibility for more than just head knowledge or feelings in our relationship with him. This new terrain is exciting to explore, but before we set out, it's helpful to have a defined trail to take us there. Moving forward blindly is a recipe for confusion, exhaustion, and loneliness. We have to prep like we're going on the John Muir Trail.

The John Muir Trail (JMT) is a famous long-distance hiking trail in eastern California. Stretching 211 miles through the rugged Sierra Nevada mountains, the JMT is considered one of the most rewarding and challenging hikes in the United States. Every year, around fifteen hundred people attempt to hike the trail, which takes twenty to twenty-five days to complete for the average hiker.

To succeed on the JMT, you must plan. Specifically, you must plan for food. The trail is a little too long for the average hiker to carry enough provisions to complete in one straight shot. Packing enough food for twenty days is too cumbersome and heavy. To address this, the JMT contains five resupply points where you can mail five-gallon buckets filled with food and other consumable items ahead of you to be picked up while hiking the trail. Utilizing these strategically located resupply points will ensure that you are able to refill, restock, and reenergize for the next portion of the trail.

To access these supply points, you must remain on the trail. The JMT is a specific route with specific checkpoints along the way. Properly navigating the trail is not only environmentally friendly; it's necessary for survival. If you stray from the trail, you won't reach your resupply points, which could put you and your crew in a precarious situation. Staying on the trail guarantees your best chance at successfully completing the hike.

Pathways like the JMT restrict our movement *for our success.* They direct our steps to benefit us. Where some people view restrictions as oppressive, hikers view them as helpful and necessary pathways to the desired destination. We sometimes like to blaze our own trails with God and experiment, but the Bible does describe a specific pathway to knowing God that we can walk to get to that destination safely.

Before we even get into that, we need to talk about relationships in general because what we understand about the nature of relationships will determine the path we choose to approach growing our relationship with God.

There are many things that go into describing the characteristics of relationships, but I will be focusing on three. Real relationships *take time,* they are *non-linear,* and they are *dynamic.*

The deepest, most intimate relationships take lots of time. You can't microwave relationship with another person. The amount of time you put in is the level of intimacy you receive. I have been married for just over fifteen years, and I can tell you that the depth at which I know my wife surpasses all my other relationships by light years. We can't grow close with someone unless we spend time with them. There are exceptions to every rule, but most relationships take invested time to *build* relationship with others and God; it doesn't usually happen overnight.

Throughout the time relationships take to build, expect lots of ups and downs. Sometimes, hanging out feels effortless and light, but eventually that might give way to darker periods—maybe bouts of anger, resentment, or deep hurt. And interwoven throughout all those seasons will be the mundane—a coasting of sorts, when the relationship just feels uneventful and dare I say it, *normal.* True relationships are non-linear. They don't just keep on improving at a positive rate. They move up, down, backwards, forwards, in circles, every which way. Those who assume otherwise will be sorely disappointed.

Relationships don't always follow a positive trajectory because they take two different people to make them up. This might sound obvious, but you need two people for connection to happen. What's less obvious is that these two people are different. I find God's design of marriage slightly humorous because most of the marriages I know are made up of two completely different people. I mean *completely different.* Opposites really do attract.

Real relationships are dynamic. People are different, and it's this difference that enhances connection. Two different personalities relating to each other result in a give and take, challenge and response, ebb and flow. This dynamic nature provides real depth and connection. It's good that my wife and I are not the same person; life is more colorful that way.

I don't think it's wild to imagine our relationship with God including these three characteristics as well. Cultivating relationship with our creator will take time. Following Jesus will include periods of growth and seasons of stagnation. And as hard as we might try, we will never be exactly like Jesus; there will always be glaring differences in our character and his.

In reality, most long term, established relationships are ten percent exhilarating and ninety percent routine. Relationships of substance are not like a sitcom. With Jesus, some of us feel this low-key pressure to make all our experiences with him extraordinary or powerful. If our walk with Jesus feels boring (or "mid" as the kids say right now), then something *must* be wrong. We should *feel* something profound when in communion with Christ. When we don't feel it, or we're worried we won't, we put stage lights and fog machines in our sanctuaries. We turn the lights way down low and hire production managers to oversee the feel of Sunday service. We gotta feel something, right?

It's also interesting that we only expect positive encounters with God. Many of the recorded direct encounters with God in the Bible were less than pleasant. Many of us assume that if Jesus walked into our rooms right now, we'd be filled with this light, airy, peaceful happiness as we float into a blissful dream state, but the Bible often places *fear* as the dominant emotion when God came near. God also spoke to people many times to rebuke or call out sin as well. Genuine relationship is dynamic, including with God.

Deep, meaningful human relationships take time to solidify, they move up and down with regards to feeling, and they involve two fundamentally different people whose differences are their strength. Our relationship with God is no different. Our goal is deep, genuine relationship with God. To know him and be known by him. *Yada.*

I have never met you, I don't know anything about you except for one thing: *You are not at the destination.* No matter how long you've been following Jesus, no matter what you feel (or don't feel), no matter what theological background you are or how old you are, you have not arrived at the depth of relationship Jesus has for you. This is because there is no limit to knowing Jesus. He's always better, there is always more to encounter. So please do not view this book as a magic pathway to some vague but wonderful destination. Rather, it operates more like a compass recalibration, pointing the way to the infinite depth of relationship with God.

With regards to knowing God, there is no final destination, only the journey toward it. And in our journey of knowing God, we need a bridge to get us going in the right direction.

Have you ever watched kids playing soccer?

It's hilarious. My kids are currently in a summer soccer league put on by the city of Minneapolis. Every Monday and Wednesday night during the summer, we strap on the shin guards, lace up the cleats, and pack up our white Chrysler Pacifica and head out to the field where dreams are created or where they come to die. It's a sacred place where blood and sweat mix to fertilize the hallowed ground of competition.

Maybe I'm being overdramatic here.

The kids are trying their best, they really are. But the gameplay is what you'd expect from a bunch of six-year-olds. There's no strategy, defense is non-existent, and the goalkeeper is busy picking dandelions in front of their net as the ball goes whizzing by.

But after each game, after parents have witnessed horrendous displays of the sport…we celebrate our kids.

No matter what happened out on that field, we shower praise and encouragement on our little soccer stars. We hand them popsicles, give them pats on the back, and offer to carry their gear back to the van. We make sure that they know we are proud of them.

Why is this? Is it because they actually played a real, competitive, entertaining game of soccer? Nope. We are doing this because we want to *build bridges*.

Our over-the-top level of praise is meant to give our kids the feeling that they actually accomplished something great. The gesture is intended to instill positive feelings in them about playing the sport. We want them to associate playing soccer with happiness and confidence.

Behind it all, the idea is to create space in their hearts for future love of soccer (or teamwork). By acting like soccer equals positivity, we hope to build a bridge in their brains that encourages them to do things in the future like contribute as a part of a team, work hard for a goal, and be active.

It's not about how they actually played the game, but when they're ready for more mature levels of soccer in the future, they will take their present, attainable experiences and package them in a way prepares them for greater, more meaningful moments.

To *build bridges* means to *practice experiencing something now* that will prepare you for *experiencing something greater in the future*. It's sort of like a placeholder for a real thing which will come later.

All learning is essentially bridge building. 2+2 is bridge building. It introduces the bridge of combination, of simple addition, so that one day, that child can solve 20+20, and then 200+200.

Praying simple bedtime prayers is bridge building. Yes, the prayers are simple and choppy, but their purpose is not to be super complex and theological but to introduce the bridge of prayer as a concept with the hopes that over time, our children develop a robust prayer life on their own.

In learning to find and deepen our relationships with God, we need bridges too. Things that engage us with him in bigger and more consistent ways. A bridge that supports us to know and be known. Experiencing and being experienced. Loving and being loved.

If our bridge includes these elements, it will create categories in our hearts and minds for real relationship with God as we continue down the road of life. This is what we are after. Real, deep, vibrant relationship with God. The kind of relationship Jesus wants for us.

My central thesis is this: the bridge God has designed to bring you closer to him is a *personal commitment to a small group of united people who are focused on living like the family of God.* By seeing God's intentions walked out by others we love, we build associations between those actions and attributes and God himself.

Keep that definition in your mind somewhere for now. There will be a quiz on that later.

The love of God is hard to experience without having some sort of idea of what love is in the first place. Like Forrest Gump, we need to know what love is to help us recognize it. Relationship with the family of God can provide that experience. God has set this all up in such a beautiful way, but there are a couple things to note here:

First, *devoting yourself to the family of God has nothing to do with your ultimate salvation.* It's only through faith in the life, death, and resurrection of Jesus that we are saved. This faith alone shifts our relationship to God from one of strife and conflict to harmony and peace. We don't "add" to the work of Jesus by devoting ourselves to living in Christian community. My apologies to all those high-achievers out there, but we can't earn extra credit with Jesus by committing to a deeper level of involvement with other believers.

Second, *devoting yourself to the family of God does not guarantee that your relationship with God will grow in intimacy.* Aside from salvation by faith alone, there are no guarantees in the Christian faith. If anyone told you that reading this book and practicing its principles was a surefire way to grow in relationship with God, they would be lying.

While not a guarantee, I do believe that committing yourself to be an active participant in a small group of believers is a great bridge that checks all the boxes that we outlined earlier. Devoting yourself to a small group of like-minded believers provides lots of opportunity to know and be known, to experience and be experienced, and to love and be loved, which provides a template for what a relationship with God might look like.

Nobody is born into rich, intimate relationship with God. It's practiced over a lifetime and with a community of people. The way we can practice relationship to God is by relating to his people. It's by choosing to live like the family of God with other people that we learn how to know others and be known ourselves, experience others as well as allow others to experience us, and love others as well as allow others to love us. This experience with the family of God can move us along in our ultimate goal of knowing and relating to God himself.

This sounds great and all, but like with lots of other things, our western culture has a few barriers that tend to keep us from really investing our time, energy, and love with other people. One of those barriers is individualism.

Remember hairspray Matt from Chapter 1? I need to tell you a few more things about him. Underneath the overly styled hair and wool argyle sweater was an incredibly self-sufficient intro-verted individualist. I still am this to a certain degree today.

I am an introvert. I get my energy from being alone. I enjoy self-reflection and the silence of early mornings by myself. If you gave me the choice to call up anyone on earth to hang out on a Friday night, I would call myself and we'd have a great time.

While you may or may not identify with being an introvert, I'm willing to bet that most of, if not all of you, identify to some degree as an individualist. Rugged individualism is an American invention on the same level as baseball and apple pie. The term was first associated with the pioneer lifestyle on the American frontier of the seventeenth and eighteenth centuries. At that time, there really was no one else; you were on your own in the vast, unforgiving wilderness, and you needed a certain amount of "grit" to survive and protect your family. President Hoover popularized the phrase in 1928 as he fought against a government that he viewed as overstepping its bounds by doing too much for the common citizen, which eroded the previously held virtues of providing for oneself. Rugged individualism has been woven into the consciousness of Americans ever since.

At their core, the rugged individualist is self-reliant, self-sus-taining, and without need for anyone or anything else. The rugged individualist lives by a "pull yourself up by your boot-straps" mentality where even appearing to need help is a sign of weakness. The strong, self-made hero is idealized while the weak, needy beggar is pitied.

So the question is not, "Am I an individualist?" but "How much of an individualist am I?"

Most of us, if we dare to be honest, are individualists by default. Our stomachs turn at the thought of asking for help. We secretly judge others who appear more needy than the average person. We act and talk in ways that portray strength and a certain "I-have-it-all-together" persona. We've been doing this ever since we spoke our first sentence of "I do it."

We are individualists from birth.

The point is this: Because of my God-created introversion and culturally conditioned individualism, I do not naturally gravitate toward community. I don't desire to be around other people, much less to invest my time and energy in others. It takes a lot of work to rev up my motor and head out the door to be with other humans.

But let me tell you, when I do muster up the courage and will to invest my physical time, mental strength, and emotional energy in others, *it's been so good.* This introverted individualist is learning.

The men of our house church have recently started serving outside our church together. Every month, we head to another part of town to spend time with other guys who are in various stages of addiction recovery. We read the Bible together, share our struggles and joys of living, and pray for each other over the course of two hours on a Tuesday night. I was recently talking with one of the men in our church and this activity came up. He mentioned that when he sees it on the calendar, he feels dread. There is so much else to do, so many other good things that we could spend our Tuesday nights on, that sometimes it feels hard to invest our precious hours into something that we have no control over.

But when he made the conscious (and difficult!) decision to head out the door and join the other guys in our church for a night of serving, that dread quickly transformed into a feeling of fullness and gratitude. This was because God made us to be like Jesus and to serve others rather than be served (Matthew 20:28). We become our truest selves when we serve others because we were made to be like Jesus in thought and action. This is why Jesus promises that if we lose our lives for his sake, we'll actually find them (Matthew 16:25). It sounds backwards, but if you were made for a different life, it makes perfect sense.

When we choose community over individuality, serving others over self-reliance, and the family of God over self, *we become our truest selves; we become closer to the people we were made to be.* You were made for community with others and the peace you feel alone just doesn't compare to the joy you'll feel in community with others. *You just gotta make the choice to get out there and live.*

Life is fuller, richer, and more colorful in community. And that's a lot for this guy to say. My social bandwidth has certainly been a journey, but even though choosing community is still hard for me, it's been getting easier over time. The more I choose community over self, the easier the next choice becomes.

Living in Christian community is hard. For many of us, the thought of devoting even more of our precious time to the people in our church whom we may or may not like is daunting. We all have relational histories filled with both positive and negative experiences with people. We've been hurt by people we thought loved us or excluded by the very ones we desired acceptance from. It is no small task to risk a life in community, and for some of us, it feels downright terrifying.

Abuse in the church has driven away many from the community of God. Abuse at the hands of the church grieves the Holy Spirit and is a slap in the face of Jesus, the true head of the Church. And to be clear, I am not advocating for you to return to your abuser—the church or leadership figure you once trusted—if they will abuse you again.

If the community of God hurt you, I am so sorry. That is not the fellowship I'm suggesting will strengthen your relationship with God.

When you are ready, or feeling brave one day, I encourage you to trust God to experience community again. You are capable of reconstructing your brain's associations with church, though it does take effort. Maybe it's finding just one trusted friend to process your grief with. Then grow that circle to a few people. Then over time, through the help of the Holy Spirit, let the community of God love you back into it.

The hard truth is that even when we've been hurt or discouraged from community, we still need it. The good news is that we have resiliency and hope. We can always grow, we can let out our sails again, we can make room to love and be loved.

Your brain is made up of billions of nerve cells called neurons. These cells connect and form pathways in your brain. The sum of all these pathways are what makes your brain work the way it does. From how you respond to a slow checkout line at the grocery store to your routine as you leave the house (did you remember to lock the door?), the way your neurons are wired largely affect how you act and the choices you make. It's how God designed your brain to function. Isn't he amazing?

The neural connections in your brain are like the highways of a large city. They are large, well-traveled, and wide. They are used every day, built over your entire lifetime, that make you who you are. And each time that highway is activated, it's like adding a little more width to that highway, making it wider, stronger, and more prominent in your brain.

Sometimes, that can feel a little hopeless. If your neurons are fused together in a fixed way, and those connections only get stronger, change must be pretty hard, right? Gratefully, God is an artist and when he created the brain, he made it quite complex. He created neuroplasticity.

Neuroplasticity is a fancy word for the brain's ability to reorganize its pathways based on new experiences, behaviors, and environments. While your neural pathways are stubborn when reinforced, they can be rewired and moved around.

In my case (and maybe yours, too), you can grow into loving time with the people of God more and more as you continue to choose community over self. Over time, those tiny droplets of love from others will grow into a light drizzle, and eventually into a torrential downpour. It takes time, it takes choice, and it takes bravery. Your brain has the ability to be renewed and transformed (See Romans 12:2 and Colossians 3:10).

So if you're reading this book and feeling overwhelmed or disinterested toward your local group of Jesus followers, know that *you have the ability to learn how to be in community.* Every choice you make helps the next choice to be easier. Even by choosing to send a small text of encouragement to a friend is a step on the pathway to rewire your brain to be more invested in your local family of Christ-followers. So start small. Do attainable things. Work with the neural pathways you have right now. Don't attempt to drive a semi-truck down a back alley.

What a true community of God offers is *the experiences that will transform your brain into the new creation God has already made you to be.* Here it is again. We know that theologically, God has caused us to be "born again" (1 Peter 1:3). In God's eyes, you are a brand-new person. But do you feel it? The struggle with vices at odds with the new title as child of God doesn't just go away in my experience.

The community of God provides you with the opportunities to know and be known, to experience as well as be experienced, and to love as well as to be loved. So that, over time, the experience of true Christian family will renew your mind to be like Jesus. Your brain is wired in a way that is often at odds with Jesus. Participating in the family of God can change your brain so that you act more and more like your truest self—an image bearer of Jesus.

You can grow through experience. Devotion to the family of God provides that experience.

The Presbyterian minister Fred Rogers sums it up well when he says, "In fact, from the time you were very little, you've had people who have smiled you into smiling, people who have talked you into talking, sung you into singing, loved you into loving."

Through intentional involvement in the family of God, we can be loved into being people of love. We can experience forgiveness in order to be people of forgiveness. By living in the family of Jesus, we become more like Jesus himself. God's design for living in community is so good and beautiful that he saved it for last in the story of creation.

We are often told that in the garden of Eden, everything was perfect. According to Genesis 2:18-20, God didn't think so. Adam was the only human on earth, surrounded by a bunch of land and animals. It's amazing to think that with the intimacy Adam shared with God, there was still a need for another human. And this was God's idea! God saw Adam and identified his need for a helper, someone to walk alongside him to support his role of caring for God's world.

So God made Eve, another human who was just right for Adam. Can you see it? Adam was the ultimate individualist. It was just him and God in a perfect, newly created world. Yet something was off. Adam needed support. He needed someone else to share life with. Individualism is not the ideal; community is. The account of the early church in Acts 2:42-47 illustrates this idea with challenging clarity:

> *All the believers devoted themselves to the apostles'
> teaching, and to fellowship, and to sharing in meals
> (including the Lord's Supper), and to prayer.*
>
> *A deep sense of awe came over them all, and the apostles
> performed many miraculous signs and wonders. And*

*all the believers met together in one place and shared
everything they had. They sold their property and
possessions and shared the money with those in need.*

*They worshiped together at the Temple each day, met in
homes for the Lord's Supper, and shared their meals with
great joy and generosity— all the while praising God and
enjoying the goodwill of all the people. And each day the
Lord added to their fellowship those who were being saved.*

This passage from Acts provides a glimpse into how the early
church operated after Jesus ascended back to the Father. Notice
the emphasis on "togetherness." The early church devoted
themselves to meeting every day to worship, pray, and to share
in a meal. How often? Every. Day. They shared their possessions
with joy and generosity among each other as well as with those
in need.

And what was the result? *A sense of awe.* Those early Christians
looked around at each other and felt a sense of wonder and
amazement. God was actually at work. The Holy Spirit was
actually moving. Hearts were actually changing. All as a result
of being devoted to one another.

I'd be willing to bet that underneath the general malaise we
feel regarding our walk with Christ, there is a lack of *awe.* This
elusive, mysterious feeling arises when one feels a sense of tran-
scendence, of being a part of something bigger than themselves,
of feeling wonder and amazement at simply existing. We need
regular moments of awe to provide meaning for our lives, to
keep us motivated and focused on living for Jesus.

When was the last time you felt this *awe* toward God? When

was the last time you looked around and asked yourself, "Can you believe this is actually happening?" That's what they were doing in Acts 2. Participation in the family of God can provide that experience again.

This devotion wasn't out of duty, but out of love. As we see in John 13:34-35, being a person of love is what it means to be a follower of Jesus and a member of the body of Christ.

> So now I am giving you a new commandment: Love each other. Just as I have loved you, you should love each other. Your love for one another will prove to the world that you are my disciples.

Those who *love one another* are true followers of Jesus. More than all the good things we do for Jesus, love stands above the rest. The world will know we are followers of Christ by how well we love.

This is the end goal of devotion to the family of God. This is where the bridge of devoted, communal life with others is going: *love of God and others* (Matthew 20:37-40). But before we get into the *how* of all this, we need to answer the *what*. He is so big, so vast, so limitless that it seems like the phrase "knowing more about God" is kind of like trying to drink the ocean dry. It's hard to even know where to start.

What does God want us to know about him? *What* does he want us to experience with each other as a family?

We're in luck, because a few thousand years ago, a man named Moses asked God that exact question.

And God answered him.

On an obscure mountain in modern-day Egypt, speaking from a cloud, God revealed five elements of his character that describe who he is. We will now take each of these characteristics in turn and discover how being devoted to the family of God can provide the tangible experiences of the very things God desires for us to experience from himself. They don't include everything there is to know about him, but since God chose these five to start off with, maybe we should too.

Let's have that conversation in Part Two.

PART TWO
CHARACTER

The Lord passed before him and proclaimed,

"The Lord, the Lord, a God merciful and gracious, slow to anger, and abounding in steadfast love and faithfulness!"

(EXODUS 34:6 ESV)

CHAPTER 5

NAME

THINK BACK TO the most wonderful food you've ever tasted. Think about what it was, where you tasted it, and why the thought of it is causing you to drool all over this book I worked so hard to write for you.

We've all had experiences with food that seem to transcend reality. Whether it's a home-cooked meal from someone you love, or simply an Arby's Beef and Cheddar, the taste of a wonderful meal is something you don't forget. Unfortunately, I have some bad news for you. Chances are, you have yet to taste the most incredible food on this planet. I have tasted it. Let me tell you how to find it:

1. Get on a plane and fly to Lihue, Hawaii.

2. Rent a car and get on Highway 50 going southwest.

3. Turn onto Maluhia Road toward Koloa (and enjoy the drive through the tree tunnel!)

4. Make a right onto Koloa, left on Poipu.

5. Take the second exit on the roundabout onto Lawai Road.

6. Right after you pass Prince Kuhio beach, you will come upon the Beach House Restaurant on the left.

At the Beach House, grab a table and order the Macadamia Nut Crusted Fresh Hawaiian Fish. Take one bite and congratulate yourself, because you've just experienced the best tasting food in the entire world.

Taste is a powerful thing. It seems like there is an infinite combination of them to experience. While it may seem like there is no end to the different tastes you can enjoy, scientists have actually narrowed down all the possible combinations of taste into five foundational tastes: salty, sweet, bitter, sour, and savory. It's from these five basic tastes that all the other flavor combinations find their origin.

It's the ritualistic bitterness of that first cup of coffee in the morning that keeps you coming back for more.

Even though that week-old couch cushion pretzel was as stale as a cardboard box, you ate it anyways because that sharp saltiness was too much to resist.

You secretly ate that last bite of your wife's sea-salt caramel ice cream last week because there's something about that delicate balance of sweet and savory caramel ice cream overlaid with just a pinch of saltiness that is just magical to experience (c'mon we all know you did it).

God designed your tongue to distinguish between these five basic tastes. Toward the front of your tongue, you have receptors that pick up on sweet and salty. The sides of your tongue are where you recognize food as sour. The taste of bitter or savory is picked up toward the back of the tongue. While God gave humans the capacity to create a seemingly infinite number of flavor combinations, he created the human tongue to recognize five basic tastes.

The infinite finds its origin in the basic. So it is with the human tongue, and so it is with God.

God is infinite. There is no end to his character. We are finite. We are limited in our ability to understand him. God knows this about us, so just like the five basic tastes our tongue can pick up, he has given us five basic concepts (or attributes) about himself that he wants us to know. The limitless knowledge of God finds its origin in five basic attributes.

After God rescued his people from the hands of their Egyptian slave masters, he then led them into the wilderness east of Egypt. Wilderness living was rough on the Israelites, with the whole ambiguous destination, inconsistent food and water, and threats surrounding them day and night. It was so rough that they began to desire to return to Egypt. In their eyes, being slaves in Egypt was better than this nomadic lifestyle God had provided them with.

Morale got so bad in the Israelite camp that when Moses took a little too long conversing with God on top of a mountain, his right-hand man Aaron took up a collection among the people for all their gold jewelry. This gold was eventually melted down and transformed into a giant golden cow in which the people bowed down and worshiped. Yeah, things are getting really bad.

God was understandably furious with his chosen nation but Moses stepped in and begged God to withhold from acting out in wrath upon his newly freed people. God listened to Moses (Chapter 3, anyone?) and refrained from punishing the Israelites.

Moses was in kind of an awkward spot. On one side, you have God who, out of love and devotion to his people, miraculously freed them from the Egyptians. On the other side, you have the Israelites, who seem to continue to find new and creative ways to disrespect the God who set them free. Let's drop in on the conversation between Moses and God as recorded in Exodus 33:12-18 (ESV):

> Moses said to the Lord, "See, you say to me, 'Bring up this people,' but you have not let me know whom you will send with me. Yet you have said, 'I know you by name, and you have also found favor in my sight.' Now therefore, if I have found favor in your sight, please show me now your ways, that I may know you in order to find favor in your sight. Consider too that this nation is your people."

> And he said, "My presence will go with you, and I will give you rest." And he said to him, "If your presence will not go with me, do not bring us up from here. For how shall it be known that I have found favor in your sight, I and your people? Is it not in your going with us, so that we are distinct, I and your people, from every other people on the face of the earth?"

> And the Lord said to Moses, "This very thing that you have spoken I will do, for you have found favor in my sight, and I know you by name."

Moses said, "Please show me your glory."

Moses begged God not to leave him or the people he was leading. It would be better that the Israelites stay put than to charge ahead without God with them. The trip out of Egypt had been turbulent so far, and Moses recognized that unless God's presence stayed with his people, everything would be doomed.

He then asked to see God's glorious presence. Other translations just use the word "glory." Moses wanted to see God's glory, or, in other words, he wanted to see what made God magnificent. Moses wanted to encounter the person of God, the presence of the one he asked to never leave. In verses 19-23, God told Moses he wouldn't be able to *see* his glory, but God would verbally announce his name for him. What made God magnificent wasn't going to be shown visually but *heard* as his name was announced.

Are you on the edge of your seat yet? What did God say? What makes him *magnificent*? What is his *goodness*? Why is he *glorious*? What does he want Moses to *know* about him? We read God's grand announcement of his name in Exodus 34:5-8 (ESV):

> *The Lord descended in the cloud and stood with him there, and proclaimed the name of the Lord. The Lord passed before him and proclaimed, "The Lord, the Lord, a God merciful and gracious, slow to anger, and abounding in steadfast love and faithfulness, keeping steadfast love for thousands, forgiving iniquity and transgression and sin, but who will by no means clear the guilty, visiting the iniquity of the fathers on the children and the children's children, to the third and the fourth generation."*

And Moses quickly bowed his head toward the earth and worshiped.[1]

Here it is. This is what God wanted Moses to know about him. From his very own mouth, the God of the universe selected these words to describe his glory, his essence, his magnificence.

This is what God wants you to know about him.

This section of Scripture, where God announced his name to Moses, is the most referenced passage in the Bible by the Bible itself. Many times throughout Scripture, these specific words of God are remembered and rewritten (twenty-seven times in the Old Testament, to be exact).

Exodus 34:6-7 is the John 3:16 of the Old Testament.

Do I have your attention now? These words are the basic level of understanding who God is. Feel free to do all the research on God's omnipotence, omnipresence, transcendency, immutability, or whatever attribute you'd like, but to put it bluntly, if you don't grasp who God is at his most foundational level, you shouldn't be moving on to his more complex attributes.

So here are the five attributes God chose himself, from his very own mouth, to describe at his most basic level, what makes him magnificent. Different translations of the Bible use different

---

1   The part about God visiting the iniquity of the fathers on the children is understandably confusing. I hope that after reading part two, especially Chapters 8-10 about God's anger, loyal love, and faithfulness, this verse will become more understandable. What I'd like you to notice right now is the *length* of God's punishment versus his forgiveness. God's forgiveness lasts for thousands of generations; his punishment only for a few (Psalm 30:4-5).

words for these five characteristics, so we will use a combination of different translations for our list in this book:

Compassionate

Gracious

Slow to Anger

Loyally Loving

Faithful

Notice that the things God chooses to describe himself are all relational. There are no "omnis" here. He could have listed all-powerful, all-knowing, or omnipresent. God could have chosen to tell Moses about his self-sufficiency or his perfect justice. These are all true and go into what makes God glorious.

But no. God gave us *this* list of attributes, *all of which require two people to experience.*

And because these attributes require at least two people to experience, it makes our bridge of living in the family of God all the more applicable. By rehearsing these five basic attributes of God with the people of God, we can grow and mature our capacity to know God more fully. The taste of salt can't be described; it must be experienced. This is because salt is a basic taste; it's the building block for other flavors. Likewise, we need to experience the fundamental attributes of God *from actual living people* so that we can learn how to experience those attributes from God himself. God's love must be experienced, not just theologized.

In this way, living among the family of God is sort of like training to become a chef. You taste *everything*, over and over again until your palate is trained to identify more complex flavor variations and combinations. It's a long process but over time, you acquire a highly developed sense of taste, leading you into richer, fuller experiences with the cuisine you're creating. It all starts with identifying the fundamental tastes of food.

So in our pursuit of knowing Jesus, let's return to the basics. With the help of others in the family of God, we can experience the five basic flavors of God's character which will lead us into experiencing (knowing) the infinitely greater character of God himself.

Together, by living like the family of God, we can help one another taste and see that the LORD is good (Psalm 34:8).

CHAPTER 6

WOMB

IN THIRD GRADE, my family had recently moved across town to a house in the suburbs of Minneapolis. I was now within biking distance of my school, and I was excited to show off my brand-new bike to my schoolmates. It was the first day (the most important day of the year for me). As the new kid, I needed to make a great first impression. As you are probably aware, how you do socially as a third-grader determines the social outcome for the rest of your life.

My mom insisted that she accompany me on the ten-minute ride to school, promising to follow far enough behind to prevent anyone from suspecting that this tall, gangly new kid needed his mommy to walk him to school on the first day of third grade. I begrudgingly agreed.

I rolled up to Rush Creek Elementary, feeling confident and hopeful. At the bike rack, I quietly scanned the area to see my mom standing far enough away to meet my satisfaction. As I was fumbling with my bike lock, a bigger, older kid came up from behind me, grabbed my bike, and threw it off to the side. I guess I cut in front of him at the bike rack, and he was not happy. He stared me down with a menacing look, then he started to mockingly laugh at me.

My third-grade career was over before it started.

Hot tears started to well up in my eyes and my lower lip started to quiver. Then, out of the corner of my eye, I saw someone running toward me. I looked toward the area where I last saw my mom and she was gone. Mom? *Please don't. No. This can't happen. I will never live this down.*

My mother, with her eyes blazing like fire (Revelation 19:12 KJV), grabbed the bike of my nemesis, and tossed it to the side. She stood a foot away from him, pointed her finger in his face, and defiantly proclaimed:

"You will *not* talk to my boy like that."

My mother's protectiveness came out as a result of her compassion for me. I was in need; she saw that need and acted. This is compassion. True compassion is a powerful thing, capable of setting off radical action in response. But the reason that my mother dropped everything to run to my aid was because of the bond we shared as mother and son. On that day, something real, something raw, something primal rose up in her to protect me in my time of need. It was instinctual. Her compassion was ignited because of something mysterious and wonderful, something deep and sacred.

In Exodus 34:6, we see God list *compassionate* as the first part of his name. The Hebrew word for compassion here is *rachum.*

This word is a derivative from the Hebrew word *rechem,* which means "womb."

The Holy Spirit wants us to consider God's compassion as closely linked to a mother and her child. This compassionate relationship starts even before the baby is born. During pregnancy, a mother and her child bond in a unique, intimate way. What the mother eats, the child eats. What the mother breathes, the child breathes. What the mother hears, her child hears. The child is completely dependent on their mother for safety, food, and life itself.

After the child is born, that relationship only gets stronger. The intimacy experienced between mother and child in the womb sets up for an intimacy outside the womb that transcends all other human relationships. The child's joys are the mother's joys. The child's sorrows are the mother's sorrows. The child's pain is the mother's pain.

So when her child gets messed with at the bike rack, it's like messing with the mother herself. And you don't mess with a mother.

Even God himself is compared to a compassionate mother. Listen to the following example from Isaiah 49:14-15:

> *Yet Jerusalem says, "The Lord has deserted us;*
> *the Lord has forgotten us."*
>
> *"Never! Can a mother forget her nursing child?*
> *Can she feel no love for the child she has borne?*
>
> *But even if that were possible,*
> *I would not forget you!"*

Like a compassionate mother, God is just unable to forget his children. The bond is too strong, the love too great. This is because God doesn't just *act* compassionately, he *is* compassionate.

Remember, God told Moses *his name* up on that mountain. He told Moses who he was at his core. God's compassionate, desperate yearning for his people is not just a fleeting feeling for him. *It's who he is.*

I don't know your history with God. I don't know what your deepest, darkest secret is. I'm not sure how solid your relationship is with God at this exact moment. But I do know this: Whatever you've done, wherever you've run to, however many do-overs you've asked are no match for the compassion of Jesus. His attitude toward you right now is one of intense love, intimate union, and jealous protection. Just like a mother and her nursing child.

Compassion is intense emotion for someone else, motivated by love for them. But there's more to it.

In Latin, the word for compassion is *compati* and we can break down that word into two parts: the prefix "*co*" which means "with," and "*pati*," which means "to suffer."

Put together, *compati* means "to suffer with."

Having a child is cute and beautiful and all, but as parents will tell you, it's a *sacrifice*. Mother and child share sweet moments of blissful newborn snuggles, soft coos and first steps, but it's not all easy. The mother's body is changed forever from carrying a child and giving birth. Sleepless nights abound. It's a struggle to raise a child as they consume most of your remaining time, energy, and brain cells.

A mother's compassion for her child is not just a *feeling* though. It's an *action* that flows out of that feeling. My mom didn't stand idly by while I was being bullied that one day. She ran over to protect me. *Compassion as action* is the truest, fullest definition of God's compassion for us. God doesn't just stop at feeling compassionate for you. He acts on that compassion. Here's an illustration to help us understand:

> *Sympathy* is feeling sorrow for your friend who has kidney disease.
>
> *Empathy* is the ability to identify with your friend's feelings because you once experienced a stay in the hospital.
>
> *Compassion* is choosing to donate your kidney to your friend out of your intense love and devotion to him. *To suffer with.*

God is sympathetic. God is even empathetic. But so much more than that, he is a God of *compassion*.

Compassion means moving beyond both of those words and *choosing to act on feelings of concern by suffering with the person in need.* It's the highest form of intimacy there is, literally choosing to deny oneself for the sake of suffering with someone else out of love and concern for them.

God's feelings toward you are so strong. He is longing for you with a deep, gut-wrenching level of emotion right now that can only be compared to a mother's intense love for her very own child. This is his attitude toward you at this very moment! It's a primal instinct that's essential to God's character.

Flowing from his longing for you are God's actions. We'll get to what God does out of compassion in a few pages from now, but before we get there, we need to discuss the catalyst that sets compassion in motion: feeling.

As I am writing this chapter, I'm at home with a couple of my kids. It's lunchtime, so that means I need to put on my executive chef hat and whip up some kid-friendly food in a flash. I need something easy to make, with the delicate balance of sweet and salty, mild and spicy, with rich umami taste spread throughout. I need something aesthetically pleasing, for eating begins with the eyes. Something that will tease and tickle their little taste buds. I need...

boxed macaroni and cheese, the white cheddar kind with the shells.

It's the perfect cultural fusion between the rich, historical culinary tradition of Italy with the warm, comforting, dairy-centric cuisine of the upper Midwest. A hero is only as good as his sidekick, so I will be pairing this cheesy pasta with cucumbers from our garden. The sweet snap of fresh cucumbers should pair nicely with the heavier, richer taste of the white cheddar shells.

The only problem is this: fifty percent of my children require the cucumbers to be peeled prior to consumption. So I end up not peeling the cucumbers and accepting the consequences. Whining and protesting ensue. I don't care.

Do I have compassion for my kids? Yes. Do I have compassion for them in this exact moment? Nope. Eat those peels, kiddos.

The thing with compassion is that it's in response to something. Compassion is awakened when we encounter *suffering, hurt, or need.*

Unlike our feelings of compassion, God's attitude of compassion toward us never takes a day off because we are always in a state of suffering, hurt, or need. While we may not always *feel* like we are suffering, hurt, or in need, the reality is that *we are. Always.* Let's turn to the Psalm 103 to unpack that. Psalm 103 is a Psalm of praise to God and his compassion takes center stage in verse 13:

> *The Lord is like a father to his children,*
> *tender and compassionate to those who fear him.*

David is worshipping God for his compassion and as we can see that in the context of verses 10-17, there are two main drivers of God's compassion toward us. These two catalysts are found in the three verses that come before verse 13, and the three verses that come after. Verses 10-12 address *sin*, which is the first catalyst for God's compassion.

> *He does not punish us for all our sins;*
> *he does not deal harshly with us, as we deserve.*
>
> *For his unfailing love toward those who fear him*
> *is as great as the height of the heavens above the earth.*
>
> *He has removed our sins as far from us*
> *as the east is from the west.*

David seems to connect our sin as reason for God's compassion. Compassion is hardly the first response many of us have in mind when we dwell on our own sin. For many of us, God furrows his brow and folds his arms in disappointment at the thought of our sinfulness. Compassion seems like the most unlikely response.

David seems to belabor that point here, stating that God isn't up there constantly accusing us, remaining angry forever on account of our sins. He even claims that God won't punish us for our sins or deal harshly with us.

Most of us have grown up with an overly simplistic definition of sin that frames it as just doing bad stuff. While it is true that sin is the actual, physical acts of rebellion against a holy God that we commit on a daily basis, there is also another aspect of sin to consider.

When Adam and Eve ate the fruit of the off-limits tree in the garden of Eden, sin entered the world. In Genesis 2, we are introduced to the real, physical consequences of our alienation from God due to our willful sin.

For Eve, the consequences of sin are focused on pain during pregnancy and relational strife with Adam due to a desire for control. Adam's suffering will include struggle to subdue and cultivate the earth that he was supposed to care for and protect. The cascading effects of sin are too numerous to count, but at least in this brief interaction in Genesis 2, we see God focus mostly on the *physical* dimension of sin. The body that was made in the image of God is now cursed, and the creation that was formed to be the art gallery of God's glory is now fractured and broken. God's world and the people inside are no longer in peaceful coexistence. Everything has changed.

Suffering, hurt, need. These are the "here on earth" consequences of sin. What happened back in that garden started a chain reaction of irreversible damage to God's perfect world. Sin is the cause of the general dysfunction of the world today. Sin warps our view of a good, holy God in favor of a distorted take on what is good, holy, and pure.

Sin is a cancer, and all of creation is terminal.

So when we talk about sin, we need to balance the classic "disobeying God" definition (which is true!) with the Bible's other emphasis, which treats sin more like an infectious disease we all suffer from.

Jesus even went so far to say that we are *slaves* of sin (John 8:34). This implies that we don't have a choice in the matter. Sin is the air we breathe. We are oppressed by it. We are controlled by it. We are consumed with it. Sin affects us every minute of every hour of every day.

Christian, you're in need *all* of the time. You are suffering from the effects of sin *all* of the time. You walk with a limp because of the sin in the world *all* of the time. But that's not the end of the story. Hear what Paul has to say after that in Ephesians 2:4-7:

> *But God is so rich in mercy, and he loved us so much, that even though we were dead because of our sins, he gave us life when he raised Christ from the dead. (It is only by God's grace that you have been saved!) For he raised us from the dead along with Christ and seated us with him*

in the heavenly realms because we are united with Christ Jesus. So God can point to us in all future ages as examples of the incredible wealth of his grace and kindness toward us, as shown in all he has done for us who are united with Christ Jesus.

Some people have said that the first two words of this passage are the most important words in all of Scripture. I believe it.

Against the deep black night of our sinful condition, there are the bright stars of God's compassion. You are a walking miracle because you were raised from the dead. And once you were raised up, God showered you with grace and kindness. God your Father is the most wealthy being in the whole universe, and he chose to spend all his compassion on you. It kind of takes your breath away.

So in response to the fact that you are stuck in a sinful body, fighting a sinful heart, and living in a sinful world, God offers you his *compassion*. He realizes that sin is a cosmic reality that arrived long before you showed up. You were thrown into this ocean of sin without a lifejacket or the ability to pass Level Two swim lessons. God is not waiting for you to become an Olympic swimmer. He's not sitting up in heaven with his arms and eyes crossed as you yet again miss the mark of holiness.

David, in Psalm 103, describes God's attitude toward you as more like a tender and compassionate father, who offers you his warm, sympathetic embrace. *God offers his compassion before correction, just like a good Father.* God wants to love you back into relationship with him (Romans 2:4).

The three verses before Psalm 103:13 describe our suffering

under sin as a driver of God's compassion. Psalm 103:14-16 address God's compassion from a different angle. Where the first half revealed the inescapable nature of sin, the second half addresses our *inherent weakness as human beings*.

> *For he knows how weak we are;*
> *he remembers we are only dust.*
>
> *Our days on earth are like grass;*
> *like wildflowers, we bloom and die.*
>
> *The wind blows, and we are gone—*
> *as though we had never been here.*

You're so light, fragile, and weak that David calls you *dust*. Dust has no control; it possesses no real authority (except to trigger allergies). Any appearance of strength or influence is just a mirage. You're not in control. Not of your husband or wife, your kids, your friends, what people think about you, your future, your health, your financial security, or anything.

You are incredibly vulnerable to external forces beyond your control. Not only that, but you are *temporary*. As quickly as dust settles on a countertop and then is wiped away, such is your life. Very few people had you in mind just three years before you were born, and only a few will remember you five years after you die.

I have a grape vine on the west side of my house. Growing grapes in Minnesota is hard, but for a couple weeks in mid-August, my vine is full of red clusters of sweet, juicy grapes. For two weeks, it looks incredible. But for the other fifty weeks out of the year, it's just a weedy looking mass of growth.

Here today, gone tomorrow. Life is a mist (James 4:14).

So in our attempt to fight our sin nature, in all our valiant efforts to be holy because God is holy, all the commitments, recommitments, resolutions, and promises made, we fall short.

We simply do not possess the mental capacity, physical strength, or emotional fortitude to live a holy enough life for God. We don't have what it takes to be all he has called us to be. While this might seem unfair or a cruel joke on God's part, it's actually how he designed us to function. The built-in futility we feel is actually the means we get to experience God's compassion.

In Psalm 103:14, David reminds us that *God knows how weak we are*. God is fully aware of our limitations because he designed them. It's not surprising to him that we mess up and fall short. Yet we sometimes struggle with this. Even though we know God loves us, what if he's frustrated with our (lack of) capacity to obey him and love him back?

If that's you, then I want you to take a minute here with me.

Just breathe. Take a few seconds of silence here. I want to tell you something very important.

God isn't in love with your *potential*. His compassion toward you doesn't arrive once you get it all together. God's compassion rests on you *this very moment, just as you are.*

He loves you right now, dust and all.

We've just covered two compelling focuses of God's intense compassion for us: our enslavement to sin and our inherent weakness to fight it. As long as we're oppressed by sin and as long as we are too weak to overcome it, we will be surrounded with the tender compassion of our loving, perfect Father.

What makes God's compassion really great is that it doesn't stop at feeling. To be truly compassionate means to feel *and act* out of those feelings. This is what separates compassion from sympathy. Compassion is a call to *do* something about what's wrong.

Think back to Isaiah 49:14-15 from the beginning of this chapter—the one about God being like a mother who is unable to forget her nursing child. After those words were written, God used a word picture to drive his point home in verse 16:

Look, I have inscribed you on the palms of my hands.

That's God talking. He wants to lay out the proof of his compassion, the action. The Hebrew word for "inscribed" here is *chaqaq (khaw-kak)* which means "to cut in" or "etch." It's more than just using a Sharpie to write a note. Here, God is telling his people that his thought of them is more than a passing mental consideration. God's compassion for his people is so real, so raw, so intense that his people are cut into the palms of his hands. This language is primarily figurative. God is using metaphor to illustrate just how devoted he is to his people, to you. This language illustrates how deep and permanent God's compassion is. Like a tattoo that doesn't fade with time, so is the compassion of God toward his people.

While figurative in nature, this statement is also literal.

About seven hundred years after the prophet Isaiah penned those words, a Jewish rabbi from a backwater town in Israel started to gain a following. He traveled all over Israel healing the sick, casting out demons, and spending time with the societal outcasts of that day. He preached a message that was highly controversial—he claimed that he was God's son, and that whoever believed in his message and followed in his way of living would experience reunion with God.

This man was named Jesus, and he was God's compassion personified.

He appeared highly concerned with the people that society had little concern for. He gravitated toward those with histories of vile sins, he touched those with contagious diseases, and he broke bread with those who had no money to buy their own. Jesus' people were the ones everyone else threw away.

As we study the life of Jesus, we discover God's priority on earth. Jesus is tenderly compassionate toward all who came to him. Jesus spent three years ministering on earth and those three years were marked by compassion for his creation.

The religious leaders of the day were irritated by how much time he spent with the poor, the outcast, and the unclean. In their minds, those people were too far gone, too needy, too broken to redeem. So when Jesus preached a message and lived a life that poured out compassion on those who seemed not to deserve it, he upset a lot of people who wanted to keep God's compassion for only those who looked a certain way.

So Jesus was killed. The radical compassion of God was too boundless of an idea for people to accept.

His hands and feet were nailed to a wooden cross erected high for all to see. The palms of his hands were literally pierced as he bore the weight of our sins. The compassion of God became a public spectacle—mocked, taunted, and ridiculed. He was taken down from the cross and placed in a tomb. Three days later he rose from the dead and appeared to his friends.

They couldn't believe it. Jesus was alive.

Everyone rejoiced except Thomas, who wasn't present with the group when Jesus appeared to them. Talk about historically bad timing. The others ran to get Thomas and tell him the news, but Thomas was less than convinced. There was no way Jesus was alive. Eight days later, Jesus suddenly appeared in the room where the disciples and Thomas were staying, and instead of rebuking his doubting friend, Jesus invites Thomas to encounter the truth. Read the account from John 20:26-28:

> *Eight days later the disciples were together again, and this time Thomas was with them. The doors were locked; but suddenly, as before, Jesus was standing among them. "Peace be with you," he said. Then he said to Thomas, "Put your finger here, and look at my hands. Put your hand into the wound in my side. Don't be faithless any longer. Believe!"*
>
> *"My Lord and my God!" Thomas exclaimed.*

You may believe that Jesus was the son of God, but do you believe in him as the *compassion of God?* Maybe you affirm the death and resurrection of Christ, but do you live like you deny his compassion *toward you?* Shame prevents us from receiving the compassion of God by poisoning our hearts and minds with the lie that we are faulty, broken beyond repair, or unworthy of love. Hidden, unrecognized shame has kept many from the compassion of God.

When it comes to the theology of God's compassion, we can be as bold as Peter, but when meditating on God's compassion *for us*, we can be as doubting as Thomas. With our noses in our Bibles and our highlighters in hand, we find comfort in knowing the cold, hard facts of how God works, what he's like, and what he wants from us. But when it comes to believing the truth of God's avalanche of compassion on us, we're not so sure. It's much easier to deal with the logical rather than the abstract. Jesus is inviting you not just to know about his compassion but to receive it.

If you struggle with receiving the compassion of God, look to the hands of Jesus. Envision the marks those heavy iron spikes left in your Savior's hands. Inspect the scars, imagine the horror. Jesus was killed *for you*. He endured the cross *for you*. Compassion means to "suffer with", and the cross is the evidence. We recite these words often as we take communion:

This is Christ's body, broken for you.

This is Christ's blood, shed for you.

Jesus is the compassion of God. His life, for yours.

Like Thomas, Jesus offers you his hands as *proof* of his compassion toward you. Don't be faithless but believe. God is pleading with you right now to see the great lengths he took to show you his compassion:

Look, I have inscribed you on the palms of my hands.

Look, and believe.

≈

I'm not sure what you're feeling after reading this chapter so far. I hope it's a renewed sense of God's compassion for you. I hope you're feeling God's comforting presence as you are reminded again of his deep love and concern for your suffering and need.

I gotta let you in on a secret though…after writing all that stuff about God's compassion, I feel no different. Maybe you can relate. Why is that? Shouldn't the thought of God's compassion cause our hearts to sing?

If the church today is emphasizing anything, it's God's compassion. We love leading with the message of our compassionate God, our loving God, our God who sometimes sounds more like a great boyfriend than the creator of the universe.

When we hear a message repeatedly, it loses its force. This has happened to the compassion of God. We've spent so much time on this attribute that our hearts have become sort of numb. We memorize the verses, we meditate on the words, we study the theology. It doesn't make it any less true, but just like a well-traveled trail in the woods, the thought of God's compassion seems a little, well, routine.

So let's blaze a new trail, shall we?

I'm a born and raised Minnesotan. Besides being known as the land of 10,000 lakes, Minnesota is known as the exporter of many great things like Target, hot dish, and Bob Dylan. But Minnesota's greatest export is a little something called *denial.*

I'm not sure how it is where you live, but we Minnesotans are experts at hiding anything wrong with our lives.

"How are you doing?" They ask us. We answer, "good."

Every. Single. Time.

It's fine. I'm fine. Everything is fine. Life is always good. While we may have problems, we will make sure we don't inconvenience other people with the stuff we're dealing with. We'd rather suffer silently and die than burden someone else with our problems. It's the Minnesotan way. You betcha.

To some degree, we all feel this way. It seems selfish to lay our suffering in front of someone else. I mean, what are they supposed to do with it? It seems like if there is nothing to do about it, then it's no use bringing it up. Bringing up our personal, hidden suffering is sometimes awkward and strange. But it's precisely this lack of openness that prevents us from receiving or extending compassion.

In the church, we've become experts at this. Sunday morning is not the time to expose your suffering. Now, nobody would ever admit this, but our actions reveal the truth. The music is upbeat, the announcements are happy and perky, the put-together pastor preaches an encouraging message meant to lift our souls. We meet up after the service for coffee, donuts, and conversation about light, simple things.

Even in many small group settings, the purpose is to discuss the Sunday sermon, study the Bible together, or go through some Christian book (maybe this one?). While nothing is wrong with that, it communicates a certain belief that the suffering and trial you are dealing with inside yourself is meant to stay that way—inside yourself.

If the rhythms of the church do not include space for people to know and to be known, then the silent suffering of people will go unnoticed, and the possibility of compassion will be prevented. We need to begin with a vulnerable admission: *something is wrong.*

But before you admit that something is wrong to others, you need to admit that to yourself. And, depending on your history and experience with suffering, this may be *very hard* for you. We've grown so comfortable with numbing, suppressing, and explaining away our fears, chronic anxieties, trials, and disappointments that we've even fooled ourselves into thinking that we've got it all together.

The silent suffering of that chronic pain needs to be revealed. We need to admit that behind the strong, happy face, is a painful grimace that just won't go away.

The internal disappointment over that dream that was lost or delayed needs to be made known. When something like a dream or hope for the future gets wrestled away from us, it makes our hearts hurt.

Longing for someone else to love and accept you is a hard road to walk, especially if you don't feel loved or accepted by the people in your life who are supposed to. It does no good to distract ourselves with work, superficial relationships, or the kid's extracurriculars in an attempt to gloss over the real state of our longing hearts.

After we examine ourselves and are honest with what's really going on, we can then articulate that to other, trusted people. This is called *vulnerability.*

Vulnerability means being exposed to the possibility of being attacked, harmed, or rejected. Revealing our suffering to someone else is vulnerable because we *can* experience rejection or dismissal. We've all had experiences where we have shared a need with someone we trust only to be met with the uncaring, cold shoulder of indifference.

That really hurts. We don't forget those experiences. Maybe that's why it's so hard for some of us to accept God's compassion today. We've brought our hurts to God but at the end of the day, it just feels like he doesn't care. We know this isn't true, but it sure feels like it.

The family of God can provide a tangible, real source of the compassion you've inconsistently received throughout your life when we allow it to. This requires immense and sometimes scary levels of vulnerability.

Vulnerability unlocks the gate that guards compassion. Compassion is impossible unless there is vulnerability.

God asks us to be vulnerable with others, and to steward vulnerability well. When others share their hearts, compassion is God's call to us.

When the suffering, hurt, or need of someone else is made known, it's time to *feel.* Don't skip this step. Remember back to Isaiah 49. In response to our suffering, God *feels* like a mother with her child. So what is preventing us from feeling when others unwrap their suffering in front of us?

We want to jump straight to fixing things, for one.

As a husband, I experience this often. My wife will lay out something that's troubling her and I immediately jump to solutions. How can I quickly take away this hurt or fear? What needs to change? What practical steps can I take to ensure this doesn't happen again?

I have good intentions; they are just out of order. What my wife needs in those moments is for me to understand her feelings. She wants more than just a quick fix. She wants true compassion from me, and true compassion includes feeling as well as acting.

I recently experienced a situation in which one of my kids was being bullied at the park. She came up to me distressed, hurt, and scared. I responded to her unfolding vulnerability by giving her a quick hug and then I went on the hunt for the bully.

I left my daughter alone on the sidewalk and sprinted down the street like Usain Bolt. I confronted the bullies (they paid me no attention) and returned to find my still broken-hearted daughter sobbing outside our house, all alone.

I heard the suffering of my daughter and went straight to fixing the situation. What she needed in that moment was to be present, to feel with her. I wasn't focused on *her;* I was focused on *myself* and what I felt needed to happen. When we skip feeling and move straight to action, it won't matter what we do. Compassion won't be experienced.

As we hear the suffering, hurt, and need from our friends, we can't forget to feel. In my experience, when someone exposes their pain, they aren't asking me to fix it. They just want to be heard and understood. Skipping this step and moving straight to action is most likely a result of my own insecurities with the situation, or my desire to just make it go away so it doesn't so inconvenience me anymore.

The family of God can be the place where people in pain are able to share their hurt and be met with loving empathy instead of emotionless resolution. By choosing to take time to feel, we allow the possibility of compassion to still be experienced.

Finally, after the suffering is exposed and felt by others, be ready to act. This is what makes compassion what it is. This is what should separate the family of God from the world.

The "thoughts and prayers" mentality is so pervasive in the Church today. Thinking about someone else and stopping there accomplishes nothing. Prayer can accomplish much. But God is calling you to act to comfort or relieve the suffering of others.

In other words, God is calling *you* to be the answer to your prayers over the person in pain. To bandage wounds and heal hearts is the way of Jesus.

Some suffering can't be immediately relieved by you. A miscarriage, death of a loved one, chronic pain, mental health issues, a burnt-out parent, or the relationship struggles a friend is experiencing can't be fixed by you. In these situations, you need to comfort. Spend time, listen, go grocery shopping, cook, drive kids, or whatever you think is appropriate in the effort to provide reprieve in during this time.[2]

Sometimes, the suffering a person is experiencing can be helped or improved directly by you. Think of food insecurity, needing money for marriage counseling, a single parent whose only car broke down, loneliness, or lack of basic physical needs for living. In these situations, you must act. Deny yourself and share whatever resources you have within your means with the person in need. Provide financially for someone's need, grab a couple extra bags at the grocery store, write a letter of encouragement, take your time and give it to someone else.

Compassion is action. See James 2:14-17:

> *What good is it, dear brothers and sisters, if you say you have faith but don't show it by your actions? Can that kind of faith save anyone? Suppose you see a brother or sister who has no food or clothing, and you say, "Good-bye and have a good day; stay warm and eat well"—but then you don't give that person any food or clothing. What good does that do?*
>
> *So you see, faith by itself isn't enough. Unless it produces good deeds, it is dead and useless.*

Your faith is useless without compassion for the suffering.

---

2   A Pro Tip—don't ask "How can I help?" or "Do you need any help?" Instead, offer something specific like, "Can I watch your kids on Friday night while you take a break?" People who are suffocating underneath trials can have a hard time even knowing what they need or want. Doing the work of offering specific ways to help is a way to love them in their time of need.

The church is useless without compassion for the hurting.

Suffering with others is the evidence of true, genuine faith. Whoever has ears, let them hear.

When we use words like "compassion" to describe God, we can't help but look to our human experience as a reference. We've all experienced rejection as a result of being vulnerable, and that rejection hinders our ability to accept compassion for ourselves and provide it to others, and by extension, a compassionate God becomes difficult to understand and even harder to experience.

God has given his family the church as an avenue to experience his true compassion. What we receive from him, we are able to give to others. God's compassion is still accessible to the world today; he extends it to the world through the feelings and actions of his Church.

First, we need to allow ourselves to be affected by the hurting. Look at the face of the homeless man as he approaches your car window to ask for help. Let yourself feel the sadness and anger that arises when the next humanitarian crisis makes the top of the hour evening news. Stop and think why the children in your neighborhood don't want to go home at night. Allow your mind and heart to experience the painful realities of others.

After we feel, we act. We don't need to start with donating a kidney. The widow brought only two coins (Mark 12:41-44). Each day contains small opportunities to extend compassion toward others. The biggest obstacle to showing compassion is not usually feeling, it's *time*. We Americans love our precious time that we do nothing with. I know the Bible cautions us against adding additional words to the scriptures but I'm willing to bet that the Holy Spirit would agree with me that an additional fruit of the spirit could be *interruptibility*. Jesus was never too busy; he didn't hold his schedule for the day too tightly. He always had time for the suffering.

So by all means, pray for God to show his compassion to the world. But after you pray that, find the closest mirror and look into it. The person you see is God's answer to your prayer. No act is too small—from grabbing the weekly groceries for a stressed-out mom to volunteering a few times a month at the halfway house to just listen and love. Set aside a bedroom in your house and ask God to fill it with the hurting. Make a couple extra burgers for your BBQ on the patio. Help your kids make care packages for the homeless who approach your car window for help. Enter into the suffering, hurt, or need of someone else and allow yourself to become the instrument of God's deep compassion for the world.

Jesus conquered death not with clenched fists but with open, pierced hands. Not with wrath, but with wounds. Not with might but by meekness.

In a world full of evil, fraught with suffering, and infused with pain, compassion can be a powerful force for good. To show compassion is not just to be nice; it's to stand up and push back the advance of darkness. It's a refusal to tolerate Satan and his schemes, to wage war against all the things that seek to bring this world farther away from the Shalom of Eden.

To show compassion is to rebel against the forces of evil and suffering that wreak havoc in this world. It's to reject the notion that the world is hopeless. It's to stand against the suffering of other humans as the natural order of life. It's to acknowledge that human suffering is not God's will. Showing compassion is a radical, counter-cultural, on-earth-as-it-is-in-heaven endeavor.

Will you join the rebellion?

CHAPTER 7

RUNNING

I REMEMBER THE feeling when those giant wooden doors flew open.

The music from the piano filled that cavernous room, bouncing off the stained-glass windows, swirling around the tall archways. Everyone stood up and fixed their gaze down the aisle and toward the back of the sanctuary.

And there she was.

There was my soon-to-be-wife, standing with a soft smile on her face, holding a bouquet of flowers with one hand, and her father's arm with the other. She personified radiance and beauty. I was overcome with emotion, and all I could utter was a soft "wow" when I saw her there.

Bradway, how did you manage to pull this off? I thought to myself.

I'm still trying to answer that question.

Our wedding ceremony continued with all the usual things:

singing, Scripture reading, a short message from the pastor. We just stood there, looking at each other. I was very sweaty and very in love.

Toward the end of the service was our time to recite vows. This was the part of the ceremony where we promise to love, support, forgive, and be there for each other until our dying days. It was weighty, reading those vows. We had no idea what the future would hold, no clue if one of us was going to betray the other in a major way, we didn't know if one of us would die young, or develop a relationship-harming addiction. Our future was blurry, full of possibilities both joyful and hard.

As we read our vows, there were no exceptions. We didn't come up with a list of things that would void what we meant. What made them powerful in that moment was the fact we said them *without knowing* what was around the corner. Our vows were preemptive declarations of commitment to each other, for better or for worse.

In a way, our vows were the promise of a continuous *gift* to each other. We promised each other to continue giving the gift of love, even when one of us didn't deserve it. Before God, we committed to continue to give the gift of forgiveness, no matter how many times forgiveness was required. Our vows were our way of declaring, *"I know that the future will bring hard things, but I will continue to gift you my love, my forgiveness, my support, my very self, to you."*

Friends, this is what it means to be gracious.

This is what it means for God to be gracious to us.

To be gracious (to give grace) is a *state of being*. A gracious person readily gifts undeserving people with forgiveness and kindness. When God calls himself gracious, he is making a declaration of who he is by default. His general demeanor, his baseline attitude toward us, is one of grace. When we wrong God, he meets us with the action of forgiveness because he is a God of grace.

A few years back, my in-laws had a leaky faucet that needed to be replaced in their bathroom. Me, being the kind and generous man I am, offered to replace it for them. My real motivation for doing this was actually to show my father-in-law that I was a real man, worthy to be married to his daughter, but that's beside the point.

I rolled up to their house, toolbox in hand. After quickly and confidently assessing the situation, I proceeded to dismantle the faucet. So far, so good. I ran into an issue where the cold water hose connected to the house water line. The nut that held the connection in place had become fused over the decade or so that this faucet was being used. I tried with all my might to free the hose, but nothing worked.

I won't be embarrassed like this, I thought. I needed to show my father-in-law that his daughter made no mistake when she married me.

Trying one more time, I secured the wrench over the nut and with all my might, I pulled that wrench to free the stuck hose. I'm not really sure what happened next, but all I can remember is something breaking loose, my 6'7" frame flying back and hitting the wall, and water shooting out from under the bathroom sink.

I had tried so hard to free the hose that I ended up cracking the water line open, releasing gallons and gallons of water all over the bathroom floor. My father-in-law ran upstairs to find this random adult man his daughter selected for marriage drenched on his bathroom floor.

I expected a sigh of disappointment and frustration. What I was met with was grace.

My father-in-law was quick to forgive me. He helped me shut the water main off and finish the repair. It was no big deal in his eyes. He was quick to forgive me because he was gracious toward me. We had a long relationship before that fateful day under the bathroom sink, and it was that relationship that cultivated the graciousness he showed me.

Forgiveness is the paramount action that flows from being a person saturated by grace. People of grace are usually patient, unhurried, at peace, and full of joy. It's a whole demeanor marked by love, acceptance, and the relentless preference for others. All of these traits are like the hiking trails that lead to the peak of grace, which is forgiveness. The choices to release offense, anger, and the desire for revenge are what makes grace really shine.

This is why God tells Moses he is *gracious* and not just *forgiving*. If you turn back to Exodus 34:6-7, you'll see that verse six is all God telling us *who he is*, and verse seven is God telling us about *what he does because of who he is*.

In verse 6, God calls himself gracious.

In verse 7, God tells us that because he is gracious, he will forgive.

God is gracious because God is always ready to give the free gift of forgiveness and blessing on undeserving people.

It would only be fitting that an attribute so beautiful and glorious and wonderful would be illustrated in the Bible with a symbol that was equally beautiful and glorious and wonderful.

Buckle up kids. We're gonna have a talk about animal sacrifice.

After God told Moses his name up on Mount Sinai, Moses walked back down the mountain to the people waiting below. He had a lot of things to tell God's people, and they were ready to listen.

First, Moses commanded the people to begin construction of the tabernacle, which was a massive, transportable tent where God's actual presence would be housed among the people. The tabernacle was just like the four-person camping tent you take out a few times a year, except the tent rods were fifteen-foot logs, and the fabric was three inches thick in some places. But it wasn't the tabernacle itself that was special. It's what happened inside it.

After Exodus, we come to the book of Leviticus, which details the complex rules and regulations regarding the animal sacrifices that were to be completed inside the bounds of the tabernacle. There is *so much* to unpack here, much more than we have time for right now, but Leviticus 4 summarizes the whole operation pretty well.

In general, when the people of God violated his commands, the sacrifice of an animal was required to "atone" for the sins of the people. They would bring a young bull to the tabernacle where the elders of the community would lay their hands on the animal and slaughter it. The High Priest (the only one able to mediate between God and the people) would perform a ritual with the blood of the animal which included sprinkling it on various parts of the tabernacle and pouring it out on the base of the altar, where the animal's carcass (minus all the fat) would be burned.

The main idea behind this strange and gruesome practice in the Old Testament was that it made God and his people "right" again. God allowed the sin of the people to be transferred onto an animal, which would then bear the punishment for sin, which is death. Because the animal suffered in place of the people, God and his people were able to continue in relationship with each other.

In other words, through the death of an animal, the people were *forgiven*.

Forgiveness is one part of what God means when he declares himself gracious. But wait, there's more.

The summary above details what is called the *sin offering*. This offering was one of five offerings or sacrifices the priests were able to make on behalf of the people. Besides the sin offering, the guilt offering was another mandatory offering performed when someone sinned unintentionally. The burnt, grain, and peace offerings were all performed voluntarily when people wanted to express gratitude or thanksgiving.

Here's what makes all these offerings similar: They were performed voluntarily, and *in reaction to something*. While God accepted their offerings, this isn't the full definition of being gracious. A gracious person is not gracious in *response* to something; they are gracious *prior* to the offense committed against them. They are *ready to forgive*. This implies some sort of plan in place prior to the offense. God is gracious, which means he is *ready to forgive*. He's chomping at the bit, as it were, just waiting to unleash his forgiveness on people.

Listen to David as he worships God for this in Psalm 86:5:

> *O Lord, you are so good, so ready to forgive, so full of unfailing love for all who ask for your help.*

This *planning* to show forgiveness and favor is really important in our understanding of God as gracious. The five offerings we discussed earlier were all performed after the fact, but there was one special offering that was scheduled ahead of time. This special day was called the Day of Atonement.

On that day, a series of offerings and sacrifices would be performed, highlighted by a ritual involving two goats. The High Priest would sacrifice one goat and sprinkle its blood on the ark of the covenant, symbolizing God's wrath against the sins of the people, punishable by death. For the other goat, the High Priest would place his hands on its head and symbolically "transfer" the sins of the people to the goat, which would then be released into the wilderness. This was an illustration of God removing the sin from the people and no longer counting it against them.

What's important to note here is that the Day of Atonement was a *planned* day. God built a planned, recurring day of forgiveness into the practices of his people. For the Israelites, forgiveness was always around the corner because the Day of Atonement was always right around the corner. The five types of animal sacrifices were all *voluntary* responses; the Day of Atonement was a *preemptive* time of grace.

God is so ready to forgive. He is planning on it. He knows we are going to need it at regular intervals. He is planning to show unmerited favor on people who don't always deserve it. This is grace.

This concept is illustrated with vivid detail in the parable of the lost son in Luke 15. In this story, a young man took his father's inheritance early and blew it on living for himself. The son ends up broke, hungry, and homeless after squandering all his father's money. With no one to turn to, he decides to run back to his father, full of shame and regret. As he approaches the family home, we see the reaction of his father in verses 20-24:

> *"So he returned home to his father. And while he was still a long way off, his father saw him coming. Filled with love and compassion, he ran to his son, embraced him, and kissed him. His son said to him, 'Father, I have sinned against both heaven and you, and I am no longer worthy of being called your son.'*

> *"But his father said to the servants, 'Quick! Bring the finest robe in the house and put it on him. Get a ring for his finger and sandals for his feet. And kill the calf we have been fattening. We must celebrate with a feast, for this son of mine was dead and has now returned to life. He was lost, but now he is found.' So the party began."*

Are you kidding me? The father saw his destitute son on the horizon, coming home after blowing all his inheritance. Because of his great grace toward his son, the father jumped off the front porch and *ran* to meet him.

In Middle Eastern culture, this would be considered shameful. In the honor/respect culture of Jesus' time, a man hiking up his robe and sprinting in public would be considered undignified and embarrassing. If you saw an adult running down their street in their bathrobe to greet the mailman, you would probably feel embarrassed for them. Also terrified.

The father's grace is also seen in his desire to meet his son while he was still a "long way off." He was watching for this moment, *ready* to embrace his son. Furthermore, rather than letting his son slowly saunter up the pathway and sit in his shame, he makes the first move and pursues his son, even though he had every right to sit back and condemn his boy. Instead, the father embraces his estranged son.

And if that wasn't enough, the father does what any father naturally does after reuniting with their disrespectful, reckless child…

He throws a party because he's back.

Up to this point, this grace the father has shown is hard to believe, but it's this final piece of celebration that sends me over the edge. Celebrating the return of this son who selfishly wasted everything he was given? This is the pinnacle of grace. God is gracious not only because he is ready to forgive, but because after he forgives, he *blesses*. He bestows love and honor on those who return to him.

Being gracious is not saying "I forgive you...Make sure you don't do that again."

Being gracious is saying, "Whatever you have done, I will forgive it. I will always love you!"

The story of the lost son is the perfect example of the gracious nature of God. It brings in all the elements of being gracious: the readiness to show grace, the act of forgiveness, and the choice to bless. But ultimately, the graciousness of God is not found in a story, but a person.

Jesus is God being gracious to us.

Like the son in the story, we are all lost. God gave us life. We have used this life for all sorts of things that go against God's will and his nature. We have all sinned, and sin is no small matter. Sinning is not like coloring on the walls as a kid and sheepishly looking at your mom when she catches you. Sin is rebellion at its peak. It's cosmic treason. It's joining the soldiers as they spit on Jesus as he's being whipped. It's that serious.

Maybe you're looking at your judgment of others, your resentment toward your spouse, your self-righteousness, your pornography addiction, or your refusal to sacrifice your life for Jesus a little differently now.

God knew you would act like this; he knew you were going to betray him. Because he is gracious, he provided a way for you to remain close. This is what the whole system of animal sacrifice symbolized. But it was just a symbol pointing to something (or in this case, someone) greater.

Jesus was the final sacrifice. This was God's plan from the beginning (Acts 2:23). Jesus' death both satisfied the wrath of God and removed the guilt of sin from us. The day Jesus died was the final Day of Atonement. Like the running of the father—what others looked at as shameful—in the story of the prodigal son, Jesus' death looked embarrassing. It was a humiliating way to die for a supposed king.

The cross of Jesus was God running from his heavenly throne down to meet you.

If you believe that Jesus died and rose again for your sins, there is complete forgiveness (Psalm 103:12). If you trust in what happened on the cross, you can walk up the driveway of God's house, and he'll come running to meet you.

And once he reaches you, his lungs gasping for breath, he'll throw his arms around your neck, pull you in close, and say something like this:

"I've been waiting for you. Everything is forgiven. Follow me, and let's feast."

This is what it means when God calls himself *gracious*.

Being a person of grace is certainly not natural for us mortals, at least for most of us. We've all experienced moments in our lives where we needed grace from someone else only to be met with condemnation. I'd like to start this part of our conversation on grace with a "hot take":

Conflict among God's people can be good.

Grace can be shown when someone wrongs someone else. So in a way, we won't be able to be gracious toward one another unless there is some level of conflict.

Yes, unity within the family of God is the *ideal*. This harmony among brothers and sisters in Christ brings God glory and is a testimony to the world. But there is a difference between fake unity and true unity.

Fake unity is based on the *absence of conflict*. Think about your best friend. Why are you friends? If you answered, "because we don't fight," that would be a little off, right? We don't define good relationship as simply the absence of conflict. With fake unity, all the effort is directed at simply not being in conflict and in much of the church today, this presents itself as living in superficial relationship with others for the sake of this "unity."

By living as shallowly as possible with others, we can prevent conflict by simply never getting close enough to each other to experience it. Ignorance is bliss, as they say. So we keep the conversations light, about simple things like work, kids, house projects, the sermon, or how good the music was that Sunday. By purposefully withholding our true selves from others as a means of self-protection, we are able to protect from conflict. This is why shame is so insidious. People who live in shame are often the most visibly neutral because their shame prevents any sort of deep engagement. So what could look like a church full of nice, happy people, who meet every Sunday for a nice, happy service and then retreat back to their nice, happy lives could actually be a church full of artificially nice, artificially happy people who are imprisoned with shame. This is biblical unity, right?

No. It's fake, and it prevents grace from existing.

In order to show grace, we must be in an environment safe enough for authenticity, truth, and, by nature, friction. You can't forgive unless there is a need to forgive. Conflict is a natural occurrence in all true relationships. You simply can't escape it if you're close with someone.

A byproduct of true unity is conflict. By now, you may have started to get the feeling that we should embrace conflict and even desire it as a sign of true unity. Before you start stirring up strife among your friends for fun, just chill for a second and hear me out. Conflict within the security of real relationship is an opportunity for growth or a weapon for disunity. It's never neutral. When tension builds, it either drives people apart or provides a chance for even closer relationship on the other side.

It's this possibility for deeper relationship that makes conflict among followers of Jesus an *opportunity* instead of something to be avoided.

Being gracious requires conflict, and that doesn't need to be feared among the family of God. Rather, conflict that is dealt with biblically can actually be a catalyst for relational growth.

Okay, so start fighting! (I kid, I kid...)

This book is an encouragement to live deeply and intentionally with others for the purposes of growing in our relationship to God. By choosing to live like this, you will experience misunderstandings, unintentional (or intentional) hurt, and general conflict. Rather than retreating at the first sign of strife, consciously choosing to tackle the reason for the contention head on with someone else can make your relationship stronger on the other side.

Relational stress can produce relational strength.

Minneapolis is located in USDA Plant Hardiness Zone 5A. This means that compared to other more southern locales, our growing season is a) shorter and b) only suitable for certain types of plants. One February, a couple years ago, I was gazing longingly outside my living room window at the planter boxes on my patio. I was dreaming of spring and the upcoming growing season when I would spend my time tending to my raspberries, cucumbers, and tomatoes instead of being trapped inside and eating raspberries, cucumbers, and tomatoes flown in from Mexico.

I had an idea to start my baby plants inside where it was warm and protected so that when the outdoor temperatures had risen enough, they would be ready to go. I bought some seeds, planted them in loose, earthy peat moss, and set the seed tray by a sunny window. The seeds sprouted and soon after, the baby plants emerged, looking healthy and vigorous in the safe confines of my windless, temperature-controlled living room.

When it came time to move my sheltered seedlings outside, it was a joyful occasion. At first they looked healthy and vibrant, but after a single windy day, most of them shriveled up and died. In my overzealous attempt to care for and protect them, my little seedlings were weak. They had never been tested by wild temperature changes and wind. If I would have waited until the temperatures were right and planted the seeds outside, they would have had no issue thriving because they were *being tested.* Testing produces enduring growth, not just a quick burst of delicate strength.

Relationships that are not tested by conflict are like seedlings that stay indoors. They might look full and vibrant, but they have no strength to endure. Conflict provides an opportunity for grace, and *grace is strength* (2 Timothy 2:1). Think about it. If we had enough grace for everyone we knew, we'd be unstoppable. Nothing can take down a relationship in which both people have grace for each other. Being gracious is sometimes viewed as a soft, delicate attribute more associated with weakness. Nothing could be further from the truth. Grace is the apex of strength. God's grace is what keeps us in relationship with him even in the presence of conflict, and grace between two people can operate the same way.

Being a person of grace is hard, and it's a growth process which requires intentional planning. Hear the encouragement of Peter in 2 Peter 3:17-18:

> *You already know these things, dear friends. So be on guard; then you will not be carried away by the errors of these wicked people and lose your own secure footing. Rather, you must grow in the grace and knowledge of our Lord and Savior Jesus Christ.*

Peter has just finished telling his readers about the coming Day of the LORD. This was a future day when Jesus would return to bring about the restoration of all creation. A lot of time will pass until then, so Peter wants them to remain alert and on guard, resisting false teachers who wish to distract them with theological error. He then finishes up his encouragement with a simple yet slightly curious instruction: Grow in the grace of Jesus.

I find this command by Peter to be a bit strange. Growth in anything is often elusive; it's hard to work toward because it's so ambiguous. It's sort of like telling someone to grow in height. That would be an awkward encouragement for someone because you don't really control how tall you get or how fast you grow.

Throughout my life, I have been asked many questions, but there are three questions that I've had to answer the most:

1. How tall are you?
2. Are your parents tall?
3. Do you play basketball?

Yep. These are the most common questions I have had to answer over my lifetime. And if you're wondering, here are my answers:

1. 6'7".
2. No, but I have extended family members that are taller than average.
3. Yes.

I never set out to be tall. I didn't wake up one morning, stare at a picture of a giraffe and desire to look like that. I made no extra effort to "grow" to be tall; it just happened. Being tall is a combination of genetics and regular, balanced nutrition. I did what everyone else did. I ate, I slept, I grew.

This process of just putting in normal, consistent work to

grow in grace is what I believe Peter is getting at. There is no magic formula to grow in being gracious. We already have the "genetics" inside of us to be graceful people. We have the Holy Spirit—God's real, actual presence dwelling in our hearts. The potential is there, we just need to participate in the normal, everyday rhythms our hearts and souls need to grow. Sorry to disappoint you, but this stuff really isn't that insightful.

To grow in grace, we must be in communion with the one who is gracious. Through a regular diet of time learning about God's grace in the Bible and interacting with him though prayer, we take in the necessary nutrition for growth. It isn't flashy, and it certainly isn't quick. I never felt myself grow as a child. One day though, I looked back at the wall in my grandma's basement and found little faded lines that marked my height at various ages and realized the transformation. Maturity happens even when we don't notice it.

We need time with God himself because we will never be able to give grace if we haven't received it from him. Our hearts and minds need to be continually stimulated with fresh doses of grace found in the Bible and through times of communion (prayer, worship, etc.) with him. This is how we grow in grace, by spending time with the gracious one.

After we put in the work of growing in grace, we then need to actually forgive people when the time comes for it (Ephesians 4:31-32; Colossians 3:13). This is the central activity of being gracious. To forgive means to release someone from your anger, resentment, or desire to punish. The concept of forgiveness is easy to understand, but the act is hard. This is why the growth piece is so important. The action of forgiving is the five percent of the iceberg that is above water. The growth process is the remaining ninety-five percent that nobody can see.

If you call yourself a Christian, you must forgive as much as necessary (Matthew 18:21-22). As much as people genuinely repent and ask for forgiveness, we should give it. It doesn't need to be given in the exact moment, but it should be given nonetheless.

Jesus' forgiveness is the reason we are to forgive others. In Matthew 18:21-35, Jesus tells a story about a servant who owed his master the equivalent of twenty years of wages. The servant couldn't come up with that kind of money on the spot, so he begged his master to give him a little time to come up with the money. His master, being gracious, forgave all *twenty years* of his debt.

The servant then ran across someone who owed him a *single day's* wages and demanded immediate payment. The man couldn't pay the servant right then, so the servant had his debtor thrown into prison. All this over one day's wage.

The master got wind of this and was furious. He forgave his servant for twenty years of wages, but his servant couldn't forgive his buddy for a single day of wages. The master had his servant thrown into jail to be tortured. Jesus tells us that this is how God will treat those who refuse to forgive others.

Forgiveness is a distinct marker of a friend of Jesus. If we don't forgive, we'll end up getting what we gave out on earth: relentless judgment. If we live our lives just waiting to condemn and judge others on earth, God will treat us the same way once we get to meet him.

Living in close relationship with the family of God will inevitably create lots of opportunity to forgive and be forgiven. Something holy and pure happens when God's people choose forgiveness over condemnation.

But a true follower of Jesus doesn't stop at forgiving. After Paul commands the Church to forgive as Jesus forgave them, he then instructs the people to clothe themselves with love. There is no neutrality here. It's not enough to forgive and call it good. The father of the lost son didn't just say, "Cool, you're back." To be gracious like God is to lavish love on the person you just forgave.

This is a foreign concept to the world, but this pouring out of love after forgiveness is what makes followers of Jesus gracious. This could look like encouraging someone after you've forgiven them or offering to serve them in a unique way after they've wronged you. It's so counterintuitive to repay someone with love who wronged you, but it's the way of Jesus. In Matthew 5, we hear Jesus renounce our western culture's ideals of reciprocal service in favor of a new set of ideals from the Kingdom of Heaven. If someone wrongs you, don't resist! If someone selfishly demands that you assist them, do more than what's asked! If someone in need asks to borrow, don't turn them away! Love the people who want you dead! Pray for those people who desire to make your life miserable!

This kind of love seems over-the-top. It feels impossible to accomplish. It's the gracious way of Jesus. It's this kind of love that has changed lives. This kind of radical forgiveness will change the Church. Even the world.

The grace of God is other-worldly. It defies logic and preference. It's so good, but we have such a hard time demonstrating
it. This is because for all the talk and study on grace we've
done, we've simply not experienced it enough times from actual
people to have a real idea of what it is. It's hard to give what you
haven't received, and showing grace is no exception.

This explains why even in the Church of all places, true grace
seems hard to find. The Church is plagued with the same sick-
nesses that the rest of the world experiences: resentment, pride,
condemnation, the list goes on. If we're honest, the amount
of grace shown between family members of God is the same
or even less than we find outside the bounds of the Church.

We have a hard time being gracious toward others because we
simply haven't experienced the grace of Jesus. Sure, we know a
lot about God's grace. Every Sunday, we sing soaring worship
anthems about the great grace of God, but that doesn't mean
we've experienced the sweetness of Jesus' grace toward us.

Maybe the reason we have a tough time accepting the forgiveness of God is because we haven't experienced true forgiveness
from an actual person before. The thought of God's forgiveness
remains a theological construct stuck in your mind and hasn't
yet reached your heart because you have no personal experience
of it.

This lack of a real, tangible experience of Jesus' grace results in
shallow, superficial levels of grace toward others. This lack of
grace inside the church affects our experience of God's grace
toward us. We don't forgive others because we haven't felt forgiven by Jesus. We haven't felt forgiven by Jesus because we

haven't been forgiven by others. It's a vicious cycle that some of us have been in for a very long time.

It's time to break that cycle. We can be the cycle breakers of generational condemnation and judgment by devoting ourselves to living in deep relationship with one another. Living deeply will provide the seedbed of conflict in which to plant seeds of grace.

So don't be afraid. Give your whole self to the family of God. Get messy, get personal, get close enough to create the friction of conflict. And when it arises, be an imitator of Jesus and use it as an opportunity to reflect the gracious nature of our good Father. To be a person of grace is to lean into the opportunity that conflict can create. To show grace is to *run towards* someone else with the gifts of forgiveness and blessing.

So take a seat on your front porch and fix your gaze on the horizon.

Who do you see? It could be a parent who never apologized for the hurt they caused you. Maybe it's your husband or wife, needing forgiveness for the same thing as last week. Or perhaps it's your son or daughter, friend, pastor, neighbor, or coworker who has tried to use the passage of time in hopes you'll just forget.

The hurt is real. The scars still ache from time to time. What they did may still affect you in real, painful ways. Showing grace does not minimize any of that. Forgiveness is a beautiful idea, but make no mistake, it's an incredibly hard and costly practice. You may have every reason to stay seated on your front porch. Every fiber in your being may be raging against even the thought of showing grace to someone who needs it.

Even so, rise up from your seat.

Even as they don't deserve it, climb down your front steps.

Even as the hurt is still there, resolve yourself to be a person of forgiveness, inhale the deep, costly grace that Jesus has shown you,

and run.

CHAPTER 8

RESTORE

My favorite book is the Christian classic *Pilgrim's Progress* by John Bunyan. If you're not familiar, it's about a man named Pilgrim and his journey from the City of Destruction (this world) to the Celestial City (heaven). The entire story is an allegory that illustrates every Christian's perilous journey from first hearing the call of Jesus to reaching eternity with him.

Very early on in his quest, Pilgrim is weeping over a "burden" that he feels. This burden represents an awareness of his own sin. Feeling the heaviness and enslavement that knowledge of personal sinfulness creates, Pilgrim weeps over his seemingly impossible situation. He then encounters a man named Evangelist who hands him a note with these words written on it:

Flee from the coming wrath!

Evangelist is warning Pilgrim that God's wrath is coming. Like a tsunami starting in the middle of the ocean, it's only a matter of time until God's wrath will crash upon the shores of this world, destroying everyone and everything in its path. Pilgrim needs God to rescue him from his inevitable wrath.

Like Pilgrim, we need God to rescue us from his coming wrath. By placing our faith in Jesus, God will save us from himself. Faith is essentially "fire insurance" that will protect us when God finally decides to burn up all who oppose him in the eternal fires of conscious torment. Faith in Jesus is our "get out of hell" card that we show at the pearly gates while our unbelieving friends fall into a lake of burning sulfur. We strut right through the gates of heaven while the blood-curdling screams of people drowning in God's wrath slowly fade out…

Right?

In all this talk about God raining down his fiery wrath, you may have just decided to build your own fire in which to burn this book. If you haven't burned it up yet, bravo to you. My explanation above was meant to be overly dramatic (I'm trying to keep your attention, remember?), but the feelings you felt when reading those lines reveal all that I'm trying to show you here.

We are incredibly uncomfortable with the idea of an angry God.

This is mostly a problem for the Western church. There are many Christians in non-Western parts of the world that have absolutely no problem with serving a God who is capable of anger. But for reasons that I don't have time to get into, we Christians in the west get squeamish with the idea of a God who is capable of being angry.

So what do we do? There are two extremes we often will gravitate toward when trying to make sense of God's wrath. For some of us, we embrace it. We pit the angry God of the Old Testament against the peace-loving Jesus of the New Testament.

The story goes like this: God made people, and people rebelled against him. Throughout the entire Old Testament, people kept making God angrier and angrier by their disobedience. God wanted to destroy everyone, but Jesus came down from heaven and told his dad to hold on a minute. God is still very angry with us, but because of Jesus, He's giving us more time to be better people until he finally gets to do what he always wanted to do: destroy the earth in his wrath. Jesus' main message to us is, "Obey me or die forever."

This thought process embraces the wrath we see in the Old Testament and essentially views Jesus as the great "buyer of time" for humanity as God the Father is painted like a kid waiting for Christmas morning, yearning to unleash his anger on everyone.

This is true, kind of.

On the other end of the spectrum, some view Jesus' life as the ultimate expression of God's true personality, which voids all the wrath he displayed in the Old Testament. Jesus is viewed as a peace-loving hippie which is what God the Father must be too. There must be some mistake in our understanding of the mean Old Testament God. These people see the biblical story like this: God was very angry with people because of their sin but because Jesus died on the cross in an act of humility; God isn't angry anymore. The angry God we see in the Old Testament must have just been having a bad day. He isn't really that angry. So now, because of Jesus, God is no longer offended by sin. He's no longer displeased when we choose to live in disobedience. God is happy, affirming, and desiring nothing more than for us to enjoy our lives on earth. God is love, right?

This is true, kind of.

These two illustrations are meant to be a little exaggerated, but not by much. Our inherent discomfort with God's anger has been the source of much division in the Church today. The divide between theologically liberal and conservative Christians can probably be summarized by the question, "Is God angry?" While uncomfortable to talk about, we need to have this conversation because God emphasized it when he spoke about himself to Moses. He told Moses he is *slow to anger*. If we are to be followers of Jesus, *we need to face the hard truth that yes, one of God's attributes is his ability to get angry, to be angry, and to act in his anger.*

I'm not sure if you've noticed it yet, but there is an elephant in the room. While God calls himself slow to anger, there are examples in the Old Testament that appear to describe God as exactly the opposite. Sometimes it feels like God acts like an overreacting teenager, blindly sending down his wrath on people who had no chance to repent.

The focus of this chapter is on two things: the *speed* at which God's anger builds up and what his anger is *focused* on. Yes, it's true that there are uncomfortable instances where God directly and harshly punishes people, but we need to remember that the whole Bible is a connected story, and nothing happens apart from that overarching narrative. So before we accuse God of being unfair or harsh when he sometimes chooses to show wrath, try to step back and zoom out to view the whole story of the Bible and specifically, the nature of our relationship to our creator.

God's intent when he created the world was to share his love and magnify his glory. He created humans to care for and rule over his creation while enjoying a harmonious, intimate, joyful relationship with himself. God *wanted* this. He values human life, and he desires for us to flourish, to grow, and to live in harmony with him. After the fall of humanity, that reality was lost. The harmonious relationship with God was traded in for a fractured one, and people became hell-bent on rejecting the God who once offered himself and all his creation to enjoy.

Some of us can relate. We have put so much time, energy, and love into someone else only to have them straight-up reject it all. Day after day, week after week, we continue to show grace and kindness only to be met with a cold shoulder. This is the overarching narrative of the Bible: God pursuing us and our rejection of him. It's been going on since the beginning of time.

God's slowness of anger doesn't mean he never shows his wrath. It means that it takes lots of time for him to get worked up (like *centuries* of patience) before he sometimes will show it. But as we'll discover later, the focus of his anger is actually *restoring relationship*, which is our ultimate need at the end of it all.

So let's get into it. I hope that after this chapter, you'll come to understand God's anger more biblically, more nuanced, and much more precious than you think.

A few months ago, I was outside in the yard with my kids when a guy came speeding down our city street at around 60 miles per hour. After whizzing by us, he stopped in front of some apartments a couple houses down from ours. The minute he opened his door, I yelled at the top of my lungs, "*Slow down!*"

He received my public condemnation poorly, as expected. After a couple colorful words, he sped off again.

I was angry. There were kids playing all over our neighborhood and they often wander into the street. He could have killed some child with his reckless behavior. Why did this anger me so much?

I value peace and safety. There is a desire in my heart for children to be able to experience life free from danger and chaos. In that moment, as that man was speeding down our quiet city street, my values were challenged. That out-of-control car had the potential to cause harm, to destroy life, to hurt the people and things I love.

Anger swells up in defense of something. It's a reaction when our values and loves are threatened.

Angry that your kids forgot to clean up their art project? You value cleanliness and responsibility.

Frustrated that you got passed up for a promotion at work? You may value recognition and climbing the corporate ladder.

Feeling rage over the latest school shooting? Your value of peace and love of children was being attacked.

Anger is a response when our values or loves are confronted. The reason for God's anger is no different. This chapter, we are going to be spending a lot of time with Paul in the first couple chapters of Romans, so get cozy. Here's Romans 1:18-23:

> *But God shows his anger from heaven against all sinful, wicked people who suppress the truth by their wickedness. They know the truth about God because he has made it obvious to them. For ever since the world was created, people have seen the earth and sky. Through everything God made, they can clearly see his invisible qualities—his eternal power and divine nature. So they have no excuse for not knowing God.*

> *Yes, they knew God, but they wouldn't worship him as God or even give him thanks. And they began to think up foolish ideas of what God was like. As a result, their minds became dark and confused. Claiming to be wise, they instead became utter fools. And instead of worshiping the glorious, ever-living God, they worshiped idols made to look like mere people and birds and animals and reptiles.*

God is angry at the hiding of truth. He is angry that this truth is being obscured: *That he is God, and he alone is to be worshiped.*

God values his worship. He loves himself and desires his creation to love him too. Because of his value structure, God made everything for one purpose: to worship him. Literally everything, including sunsets, white cheddar macaroni and cheese with the shells, the way a baby smiles in their sleep, your team winning the Super Bowl, and the smell of coffee in the morning is meant to tell us that

1. There is a God, and

2. He is to be worshiped and thanked.

So when this doesn't happen, when we remove God from the picture and choose to value his things more than him, he gets angry. God's values of worship and thanks are attacked when his creation chooses to worship and thank other things. While this might seem self-centered on God's part, *it's actually the most people-centered response there is.*

Notice what happens as people refuse to honor God: Their minds become darkened and confused. The more we focus on worshipping and honoring the things God has made, the more we devolve into darkness and confusion. Worship of the self is like being addicted to drugs. The more we do it, the more we need to do it, and the more lost we become.

What we have been talking about here is *sin*. Sin is anything that disagrees with those two points above. The Bible is very clear about what sin does to us and God. Listen to the prophet Isaiah in Isaiah 59:2:

> *It's your sins that have cut you off from God.*
> *Because of your sins, he has turned away*
> *and will not listen anymore.*

Our insistence on not honoring God causes us to be cut off from him. When we choose to worship the things he made more than God himself, we become separated.

God values intimate relationship with us, but sin destroyed that intimacy.

God loves when his creation thrives, but sin interrupts that prosperity.

God's values and loves are threatened, so he gets angry.

But his anger isn't just because he isn't getting worshiped. God is not petty like that. He isn't pouting in heaven like a five-year-old at a birthday party whose friends decided to play a different game. Paul continues this thought in Romans 1:24-27:

> *So God abandoned them to do whatever shameful things their hearts desired. As a result, they did vile and degrading things with each other's bodies. They traded the truth about God for a lie. So they worshiped and served the things God created instead of the creator himself, who is worthy of eternal praise! Amen. That is why God abandoned them to their shameful desires. Even the women turned against the natural way to have sex and instead indulged in sex with each other. And the men, instead of having normal sexual relations with women, burned with lust for each other. Men did shameful things with other men, and as a result of this sin, they suffered within themselves the penalty they deserved.*

Paul says when people sin, they suffer *within themselves*. By engaging in activity that goes against those two points above, it's not only offensive to God, but it hurts people in the process. There will be a final judgment for people who willingly refuse to acknowledge or worship God, but the harmful effects of sin aren't just reserved for when Jesus returns.

When you go against God's will and refuse to honor him, someone *always* gets hurt. Sin destroys the fabric of God's good world, which makes God angry.

When you look at a person with lust in your heart, you're hurting someone. God gets angry.

When you don't control your food addiction, you're hurting someone. God gets angry.

When you harbor jealousy toward someone else, you're hurting someone. God gets angry.

This is why when my son runs into the street without looking, I get angry at him. I'm upset because I don't want him to get hurt. If he gets hit by a car, I could lose him. The thought of losing my boy makes me sick to my stomach. I love him so much. *I get angry with him because I love him.*

So maybe God's anger isn't so self-centered after all.

Maybe God's anger isn't just meant to punish,

but to *restore*.

When we act out in anger, it's often in the form of punishment. For the example of my son and the street, I might make him sit on the picnic table for five minutes while his siblings continue to play. I want him to associate running into the street with taking a time-out. Works every time, right, parents?

Sometimes God does the same thing. We have enough evidence in Scripture that leads us to believe God can actively punish people himself for their sinfulness. In Numbers 21, God sends down poisonous snakes to bite his people for their disobedience. That's one way to do it, I guess.

While God is certainly capable of punishing his people for their disobedience, most of the time, God doesn't directly punish us himself. More often than not, God punishes us by giving us exactly what we want.

God's punishment is sometimes letting us experience the natural results of our sin.

Sinning against God will always hurt someone. Everything, from the burnt-out business person's emotional affair at work, to the mega-church pastor emotionally abusing their congregants for the sake of their own gain, to short-tempered parents exasperating their children will carry hurt and pain in their wake. Sin is never neutral.

God doesn't need to directly punish us himself. *We'll do a good enough job of it ourselves.* We see this all over the Old Testament. God repeatedly gives his people over into the hands of other nations as a result of their disobedience. The Israelites were supposed to find their strength and protection in God, but when they repeatedly chose idolatry and sin, God let the natural consequences take over.

Ultimately, this was the reason they were all exiled out of the promised land. Natural consequences of sin lead to pain and suffering. God chose to strengthen and provoke enemy nations around Israel, and then he stepped back and let things naturally happen. If we circle back to our Romans passage from earlier, we see this in verses 24-26:

> *So God abandoned them to do whatever shameful things their hearts desired. As a result, they did vile and degrading things with each other's bodies. They traded the truth about God for a lie. So they worshiped and served the things God created instead of the creator himself, who is worthy of eternal praise! Amen. That is why God abandoned them to their shameful desires.*

Our anger looks like active punishment. God's anger looks like leaving us to bear the consequences of our sin. Well, this seems pretty bleak. Now God seems even more ruthless and petty than before. Can we go back to the chapter about God's grace?

Hold on. Here's where things start to get really good.

God's anger has a purpose: *his anger is meant to restore us to himself.* This takes place in five movements:

1. When we sin against God, he gets angry because sin separates us from him.
2. When God gets angry, he lets us experience the results of our sin.
3. When we experience the results of our sin, we suffer.
4. When we suffer, God is compassionate.
5. When God is compassionate, we return to him.

God's anger is not primarily about punishing us, but about *restoring us* back to him. This is what differentiates your kind of anger from his. In Hosea 11, these five movements are brought together as God retells the story of his pursuit of his people, their rejection of him, and his promise to take them back in compassion. Open up your Bible and read Hosea 11, then follow along:

Verses 1-4 are about how God loved his people, but they were determined to love and serve other things. Their sin makes God angry.

Verse 5 is about how God, in his anger, allowed his people experience the results of wandering out from under his protective presence. They will be taken captive by the nation of Assyria.

Verses 6-7 detail the suffering Israel will face as a result of their sin. War and violence will take over the nation as a natural consequence of their sinfulness.

Verses 8-9 describe God's compassion. Although God is angry, he will not act out of anger on his people. The reason God gives for his incredible restraint is that he is God, and not a human.

Verses 10-11 finish up the story with the relationship between God and his people being restored as he brings them back from their captivity in Assyria. They are back home with their God.

In verse 1, God gets angry. Verses 2-10 detail what God will do as a result of his anger. In verse 11, the relationship is restored. *It's God's anger that accomplishes his plan of restoration.* I bet that sentence wasn't on your Chapter 8 bingo card.

This is why back in Exodus 34, God calls his anger *slow*. This whole operation takes time. God is patiently letting this process play out. Right now, if you are reading this, you have time to confess your sins, commit to follow Jesus, and receive the compassion of God. As long as you have breath, you can use your next breath to respond to his tender compassion for you. God's kindness is just waiting at the door of your heart, just ready to be experienced. God's compassion is meant to lead you to repentance (Romans 2:4).

In his mercy, God isn't choosing to unleash his wrath at the moment of sinfulness. Rather, He's patiently waiting for you to be honest about your sins, receive his compassion in your suffering, and return back to him.

Earlier on in this chapter, we discussed how it sometimes feels unfair when God lets his anger out on people. But do you know what's really unfair? When God sends his wrath down on the innocent.

Shortly before Jesus was to be arrested, he withdrew to a forest of olive trees and prayed. As he prayed, he became so overcome with stress and emotion that his sweat became tinged red with blood. The medical term for this is hematidrosis, and it can occur during periods of extreme anguish.

While Jesus was praying there, he uttered these words found in Luke 22:42:

> *Father, if you are willing, please take this cup of suffering away from me. Yet I want your will to be done, not mine.*

Earlier language used in the Old Testament seems to indicate that the cup Jesus was referring to was the cup of God's wrath, his extreme anger. Jesus was sweating blood because he was about to experience the divine consequences for disobedience to a holy God.

While God's anger is slow, there will be a day where he withholds it no longer. A day is coming where God's white-hot wrath will be revealed against every molecule of sin in the known universe, purifying it for eternity. God will not declare innocent those who are guilty (Exodus 34:7), and those who reject God's offer of compassion will be destroyed forever. For those who respond to God's compassion with repentance, *God's anger is completely removed without a trace remaining* because Jesus experienced the anger of God on himself.

The anger that was meant for you was endured by him. Jesus died because the punishment for sin is death (Romans 6:23). So for the one who trusts in Jesus, God's anger is not only slow, but it's *ultimately removed.*

God's anger is a beautiful, terrible thing. his anger is driven by a heart of restoration, not punishment. God's ultimate goal of restoration is evidenced by sending Jesus to the cross. He endured our suffering so that we could be brought back to God (1 Peter 3:18). What greater picture of compassion is there?

After a moment of abandonment, we can experience an eternity of his love as we see in Isaiah 54:7-8:

> *For a brief moment I abandoned you,*
> *but with great compassion I will take you back.*
>
> *In a burst of anger I turned my face away for a little*
> *while. But with everlasting love I will have compassion on*
> *you," says the Lord, your Redeemer.*

If we were to weigh God's anger and God's compassion, his compassion would win out. In Exodus 34:7, God compares these two attributes in terms of time. Compared to his forgiveness, God's anger lasts only moments.

You've spent enough time estranged from God, suffering in your own repetitive sins. You've settled for bland, superficial relationship with him for too long. Your heart has been iced over for too many years in lukewarm faith.

Let his compassion thaw your heart and draw you home.

He's too angry to let you go.

❧

On December 6, 2018, Southwest Airlines flight 278 was on approach into the Bob Hope Airport in Burbank, California. The weather in Burbank was challenging at the time, with heavy rain and gusty, rapidly changing winds currently swirling around the airport. As the Boeing 737 was descending toward the runway for landing, the winds became so unpredictable that they shifted to a strong tailwind from behind that caused the airplane to float down the runway longer than planned.

After touching down one thousand feet beyond the normal landing point, the giant passenger jet struggled to come to a stop. The runway in Burbank is already shorter than average for a commercial airliner, with a dense commercial business area sitting just beyond the end of the runway, across from a major city street. Something needed to happen quickly, or many lives would be lost.

The pilots were unable to stop the aircraft in time, but a very intelligent engineering feature saved the lives of everyone onboard. At the end of the runway, there was an Engineered Materials Arrestor System (EMAS) installed. An EMAS system is a pad of soft material laid out at the end of a runway which is designed to give way under the weight of an airplane to absorb its momentum before it exits the airport boundary. It's designed to let the rogue airplane sink into its soft yet rigid surface and bring it to a stop, protecting the passengers on board and the surrounding area from catastrophe. It's a safety net, designed to capture an airplane that is headed for destruction.

We are going to spend the rest of this chapter building an EMAS system for the runway of our hearts for when our unrighteous anger toward someone else starts flying down it. We need to design something that will absorb the energy of our uncontrolled anger before it harms us or other people. If we can do this, we will have an easier time restoring our relationships because we will spend less time self-sabotaging them. Slow, restorative anger. It's the way of Jesus and it must be the way in the church.

The previous chapter was about being gracious, and that is a great goal. But no matter how much we try to grow in grace, we will still get angry. We can be people of grace and people of anger; they're not mutually exclusive. Not all anger is bad, either. God gets righteously angry, and humans have that capacity too. Righteous, God-honoring anger has done a great deal of good in the world. Injustice, oppression, and evil against the innocent should make you angry. It makes God angry. The problem is, for as much as we demonstrate restorative anger, we humans tend to gravitate toward punitive, violent, self-centered anger a whole lot more frequently.

The church is fertile ground for this destructive anger to take root. Lots of relationships, lots of expectations. My friend recently calculated that in his family, there were twenty-one different person-to-person relationships. That's a lot of opportunity for people to be misunderstood, to store up resentment, to experience anger. In his family, it's not about seven people being happy; it's about twenty-one different relationships staying united. When you look at it that way, the fight for unity seems a lot more difficult.

Apply that to your church. There are probably hundreds if not thousands of separate relationships that make up your church family. If you do the math, it's not a matter of *if* someone will be angry with someone else, but *when*. There's just too much potential for strife among people. Which is why the Bible has *a lot* to say about anger among followers of Jesus. It's no small thing. From our discussion so far, here are the two main ways our anger differs from God's:

1. Our anger often flows from a selfish desire to inflict pain and revenge; God's anger carries with it the hope of restored relationship.

2. Our anger is often quick and self-focused; God's anger is slow and other-focused.

Fundamentally, our anger is different from God's. Because of our sin, we get angry for the wrong reasons and act out in the wrong ways. So for the rest of the chapter, we'll focus on how to *do anger well in the church*. This might seem like a weird goal, but frankly, I'm done trying to prevent anger from happening in the first place. We need to focus on being angry while not sinning (Ephesians 4:26). While anger within the church not ideal, Scripture seems to indicate that feeling angry is not a sin, but acting sinfully out of anger is. *We want our anger to be restorative and slow like God's.*

So again, our goal is not to be free from anger. Our goal is to slow our unrighteous anger down in hopes of neutralizing it before we do something we'll regret, before we sin against each other. We need a game plan to rise above our feelings of anger, name it for what it is, and peel back any unrighteous thoughts, motivations, or beliefs. By doing so, we'll honor God and save others from ourselves.

When the reserves of grace are spent, when someone catches us on a terrible night of sleep, when the kids are just doing too much, or when your mother has passively insulted your life choices for the last time, there is a natural gravitation to anger which, left uncontrolled, can turn sinful. This feeling isn't bad; it just needs to be dealt with. If you can remember back to the previous chapter, growing in grace was primarily an isolated, internal activity. To grow in the grace of God, we need to spend time with him. Because the Bible often links forgiving others with the forgiveness of Jesus, we need to understand the forgiveness of Jesus in our own hearts.

Adopting an isolated, internal approach to slowing our anger down is exactly what NOT to do. Anger is an emotion that wants to be kept inside, unprocessed. If we resort to stuffing it, packing it away like a hoarder in the recesses of our heart, it will calcify until our reality is distorted. Resentment is much harder to root out than anger itself.

Our strategy to absorb our unrighteous anger needs to allow for *release* of that anger. It can't stay in. And no, the person who set off our anger can't be the first person we release our anger to. We are not ready for that yet. The first person we must release our anger to is God himself.

David is our example in this. Several of the psalms included in the Bible deal with anger, with Psalms 35, 69, and 109 being the most intense. These sections of Scripture are called *imprecatory* psalms, and they are the psalms your worship leader skips for the call to worship. David is pulling no punches here, asking God to kill his enemy to render his children fatherless. He even goes as far as to ask God to make the creditors of his enemy require immediate payment. In modern language, David is praying that the bank that holds your car loan would suddenly demand full payment for your car. You gotta hand it to David; he's being creative. Even though much of David's anger could be classified as righteous, we can still learn from his act of taking it to God.

God needs to be the first person we take our anger to because he is the safest person to go to. Unprocessed anger has a tendency to be sharp—too sharp for other people. As David shows, God can handle it all—the rage, the disappointment, the fury. He is not taken aback, nor is he surprised, because he has already seen your heart. Like we learned back in Chapter Three, He's inviting you to tell him everything he already knows.

Surprisingly, this act of taking our anger to God first can do wonders for our own hearts. I'm sure you have experienced the freeing feeling of just processing something out loud, only to come out other side feeling lighter and more clear headed. As we turn over what's bothering us, we can see where we are being inconsistent, where we need to show grace. It just requires us to relax our tight jawbones and tell it to God.

For the past year or so, I've been trying to include a rhythm of confessing to God what (or who) is causing me to feel anger. Once or twice a week, I get up before my family and take Charles Barkley, my really cute but really dumb Golden

Retriever, for a walk. During this walk, I quiet my heart and really try to feel what is lurking beneath the surface of what I'm aware of.

Who is causing me frustration?

Who do I feel the tinge of anger at?

What person is on the last straw of my compassion right now?

Why do I feel angry or frustrated at them?

Is this anger righteous or unrighteous?

After processing for a bit, I release those people and the anger and frustrations they bring to the LORD as best I can. I remind myself he is God, not me. I find that after doing this, my levels of anger decrease, and I am able to see these people in a more compassionate light. I try to do this as often as necessary, but it averages out to be around a few times a week.

This practice is called *benevolent detachment*. It's benevolent because it's a way to actually love my neighbor. No one wants to experience angry and frustrated Matt. It is an act of love to release my anger toward other people. It's detaching because it requires me to "rise above" my feelings and name what is true. Often I need to be reminded that the people I'm frustrated with are broken people who need the mercy of Jesus. This requires me to "detach" from my feelings of offense to see the clear, true reality that they are, like me, sinners in need of grace.

So try it out. You can even practice this with what makes you anxious, fearful, or worried. This practice can also help you process feelings of anger toward less concrete things like anger at systemic injustice, oppressive powers, or evil groups of people you have no relationship with. Directing your anger and sadness to God in these situations is called lament, and it's a totally biblical practice. I trust that after a few days, you'll find this practice to be a great way to dig out the root of bitterness from your own heart before it spreads (Hebrews 12:15).

After we have brought our anger to God, we might be ready to bring it to the person our anger originated with. But not always. For deep hurt, we may still need time to process and release before we approach the person who hurt us. This is where we can bring our anger to another trusted person. This person might be a good friend, therapist or counselor, pastor, mentor, or anyone who knows us well and is mature enough to help us walk through our feelings of anger.

I can't stress this enough: They need to be mature. It will do no good to process our anger with someone who will just agree with our side of the story (Proverbs 27:6). We need people in our lives who are able to see, objectively (not affected by emotions), our situations and reasons for our anger. Eric with the peanut butter cup was that person for me. I don't remember everything I said that afternoon, but I can imagine there was a fair amount of self-pity, a me-against-them attitude that Eric had to listen to. When I'm angry, I tend to play the victim; that's the card I lay down. If there was an Academy Award for best male actor as the victim of everyone else's problems, I would win. I know this about myself because other people (my wife, Eric, etc.) have shown me.

As a twenty-five-year-old, I thought I was the victim of everyone else's sin. As a thirty-six-year-old, I still do that, but to a much less extent, which makes life for everyone around me much better. This is all due to processing my anger with other people who are uninvolved with the situation I'm angry about. God has refined my heart using other people. (Hey, that's kind of the point of this book!)

Finally, after we have taken our anger to God and then to another, trusted person, we are ready to confront the person who caused our anger. Depending on the specific situation, there may be a lot of time spent in the first two steps. This isn't a checklist, and just because we spent time processing with God and others doesn't mean we're ready to talk to our offender yet. It might take hours, days, weeks, months, or even years of intentional processing with God and others before we are ready approach the person who hurt us. The timeline depends on the depth of hurt and anger we are experiencing.

There may be a lot of pressure to rush this attempt at reconciliation, but unless our heart is right toward the offender, continue to process. What's not okay is simply ignoring the anger and hurt. That does nobody any good. The period of time, however long it may be, between the offense and reconciliation should be used for conversation, lament, and dialogue between ourselves, God, and other people.

When the time is right, we need to close the loop on our anger with the person we were angry with. I have witnessed the power of a neutral mediator in this case. We don't need to complete this step alone. Sometimes, a neutral third party helps keep the conversation on track and God-honoring. This trusted, mature person would be responsible for just being present during the conversation, being on the lookout for any signs of sin or crossed boundaries from either side, with the authority to shut down the conversation should it turn unhelpful.

Living closely with other people (even followers of Jesus) will cause strife, misunderstanding, and hurt. It's not the ideal, it's just natural. When that happens, we need to remove ourselves from the situation and begin the process of releasing our anger. Unlike growing in grace, processing anger requires release.

First, we should take our whole selves with all the raw emotion we're feeling and bring it to God. He can handle it. Feeling anger is not a sign of weakness or doubt. He is mindful. After pouring our hearts out to God, we should process our anger with another trusted friend. God has given us people in our life who have the ability to see things from a neutral perspective. Allow these people to love us by offering their perspective on things, which should include steps *we* can take to work for reconciliation. Finally, and only when our hearts are truly ready, we are ready to release our processed, controlled anger to the person who hurt us in an attempt to close the loop on reconciliation.

This process of taking our unprocessed, uncontrolled anger and turning it into a means of reconciliation is how we, as people in the family of God, imitate the slow, restorative anger of God. Like a delicious Texas brisket, slow-cooked anger brings Jesus joy. Read what Paul wrote to the church in Philippi on this subject in Philippians 2:1-4 (ESV):

> *So if there is any encouragement in Christ, any comfort from love, any participation in the Spirit, any affection and sympathy, complete my joy by being of the same*

mind, having the same love, being in full accord and of one mind.

Paul loved the group of people living in Philippi. Individuals loving Jesus is great. People participating in the activity of the Holy Spirit is wonderful. For Paul, collective unity of the people that made up that church was the next big goal. To hear that the messy Philippian church was of the same mind and loving the same things would bring Paul a full, complete joy. Jesus is interested in your personal relationship with him but more than that, Jesus wants a unified church full of individuals who love and obey him. A church that is able to demonstrate slow, restorative anger is unstoppable. This bond is strong enough to weather anything. You have a chance to model this on a micro level with your own spiritual family.

Cultivating a heart of slow anger is incredibly hard. We've all been on the receiving end of fast, unrighteous anger. Maybe it was a parent growing up, a trusted friend, coworker, or even a random stranger. I'd be willing to bet that most of the anger we have been exposed to in our lives has been unrighteous, and it hurts.

So when we read about God's anger, we can't help but draw upon our negative experiences of sinful anger from other people. Maybe that's why we get so uncomfortable talking about a God who gets angry. In our real, lived experience, much of the anger we experienced was hurtful, fast-acting, meant to punish, and possibly abusive. God can't be that type of angry, right?

He's not. God's anger is much different from human anger. God's anger is restorative—meant for reconciliation and not for punishment. His anger is slow to develop, giving people time for confession and repentance.

There's such a difference between the unrighteous anger we've experienced first-hand and the righteous anger we read about in the Bible. The family of God can provide opportunity to both exercise and experience righteous anger. Anger seems ominous, both to talk about and to experience. It's a charged emotion, colored by our often-negative past experiences with it. Addressing anger is intimidating at first because of its mystery. How do we approach something we don't know very much about?

A few years back, my family had the opportunity to fly in a hot air balloon over southern Arizona. At first, it was a little scary, floating so high in a wicker basket with nothing but a giant bag of hot air keeping us in the air. But after a while, it became peaceful, surreal, and magical. The thought of flying changed from intimidating to refreshing and rewarding. Experiencing restorative anger is often similar. At first it seems threatening, but it ends up being refreshing and unifying.[3]

By devoting yourself to the family of God, opportunity for anger will inevitably arise. By building a process for slowing our unrighteous anger down, we can provide space and time for our anger to be *processed in community* which leads to restoration and not resentment. This opens the door for reconciliation. This is the fight for unity. This will bring Jesus glory as his church processes anger well. By committing to handle anger in

---

3   By the way, our hot air balloon ride ended with a terrifying crash as the basket impacted the ground at the wrong angle, which sent my seventy-five-year-old grandma flying out of the basket and onto the rocky Sonoran Desert floor. Metaphors only go so far...

a God-honoring way in the church, we'll get a clearer picture of God's righteous anger as illustrated throughout the Bible.

So let's stop pretending we're not angry. In a world that is quick to anger and ready to lash out, we can point to an ancient, beautiful way of living Jesus taught us that still acknowledges our anger but processes it safely and ultimately uses it for restoration. Imagine a world that uses anger not to punish or exact revenge but harnesses all its power and emotion for our flourishing and God's glory. Think of the limitless possibilities that arise when anger is not something to be avoided, but something to press into and used for good.

This is the restorative power of slow anger in the Kingdom of God.

CHAPTER 9

BOUND

Ah, Valentine's Day.

Whoever the corporate genius was that came up with a random day to celebrate love and to spend lots of money, I salute you. The Bradway family loves Valentine's Day. My wife got up early and made heart-shaped waffles for the kids, and she hid little love notes in their school backpacks. I stopped by the flower shop during the day and bought a bouquet of overpriced roses for my bride, as well as a couple smaller bunches for my two little girls. I took my wife out to a nice little restaurant for lunch, and we enjoyed just being together, acting like the kids we were when we first met. Call us cheesy, call us gullible, but we heart Valentine's Day.

Keeping in step with our immature love for February 14, we decided to finish it off with a classic tradition: watching a cheesy romantic movie together. As far as movies go, I am much more of an indie film guy than a corporate romance lover, but for this day, and for this woman, I made an exception. I'm not sure what generation you're from, but for a couple of people in their thirties, there was one romantic movie from the mid 2000s that seemed to be everyone's favorite: *The Notebook*.

The Notebook is a story about Noah, a poor laborer who wins the heart of Allie, a rich yet down-to-earth young woman who has no trouble seeing past Noah's lack of wealth or influence. She falls for him, and the majority of the movie is about their oftentimes volatile relationship that ends with them sticking together. Early on, Allie's parents reject Noah because of his poverty, and the stress of the relationship causes them to break up. Noah goes off to war, Allie gets engaged to someone else, Noah returns and wins Allie back again. It's a story of love between two unlikely people, illustrating the power of commitment and loyalty against all odds.

The most powerful scene comes near the end of the film where we see both Noah and Allie at the tail end of their lives. Allie now lives in a nursing home because of her deteriorating mental state. Her dementia has caused her to forget who Noah is, which is heartbreaking. Noah doesn't care though, and he regularly shows up to the nursing home to read Allie a book she wrote about the story of their relationship. Day after day, Noah continues to read Allie their story in hopes she'll remember and return to him mentally. She's still there, Noah just has to help her remember.

Their extended family pleads with Noah to just stop. It's no use trying to bring Allie back by reading to her. The doctors also think Noah's strategy is useless. He just needs to accept the fact that Allie is gone, and she isn't coming back.

What they don't know is that Noah is bound in love to Allie. He made a commitment to her and that commitment defies logic. Love makes you do strange things, doesn't it? It's this insistence, this devotion to Allie no matter what happens, that makes Noah's love for Allie extraordinary. Noah can't let her go; it's impossible for him.

The movie ends with Allie finally coming back, if only for a few minutes in a hospital bed. Noah climbs in bed with her, and they end up dying together while holding hands that night.

I'm not crying, you're crying.

The depiction of Noah's "against all odds" love for Allie is powerful, and it's borrowed from the Bible. *Hesed* is the Hebrew word for this incredible, binding love in the Old Testament. It's a complicated word, full of meaning. We need to consult a commentary to help us understand it further.

For me, there is one commentary that stands above the rest. I have frequently used it in my times of need, and it has always come through. It's theologically rich, easily applicable, and simple enough for children to understand it.

Well, uh, maybe that's because it's written for children.

The Jesus Storybook Bible by Sally Lloyd-Jones is my favorite commentary. Lloyd-Jones does such a beautiful job telling the stories of the Bible in a way that they all point to the real story, Jesus himself.

I'm holding my tattered copy of *The Jesus Storybook Bible,* and I can't help but think of all the memories snuggling up my children and reading together. The cover was torn off long ago, probably by an angry toddler refusing to go to bed, but the sentiment remains the same. The stories we shared together were so rich, so full of meaning, that I was even prompted to worship often as we read these simple renditions of such powerful truth.

How do you begin to describe God's love to a three-year-old? Rightly understood, the love of God is indescribable. We can't even begin to fathom the dimensions of this limitless love. Listen to Paul confront this beautiful mystery in Ephesians 3:18-19a:

> *And may you have the power to understand, as all God's people should, how wide, how long, how high, and how deep his love is. May you experience the love of Christ, though it is too great to understand fully.*

How do you describe the indescribable? How can you understand the unfathomable? *What is the love of God?*

Some translations use the word *lovingkindness.*

Some use *mercy.*

Our translation calls it *steadfast love.*

The Hebrews used *hesed.*

Sally Lloyd-Jones called it *God's never-stopping, never-giving up, unbreaking, always and forever love.*

We'll simply call it *loyal love.* I can't wait for you to read this.

Hesed is the Hebrew word used for *loyal love* in Exodus 34:6. This word, like many Hebrew words, is not directly translatable into English. In fact, the word *hesed* is used around 250 times in the Old Testament translated some 160 different ways throughout all the English translations. Put those two facts together and you have one word with a whole lotta meaning and importance packed into it.

Hesed means love, but it means much more than that. *Hesed* implies a love that is combined with generosity and commitment. It's God's loyal, steadfast, continuous, covenant-making, promise-keeping, generous love that is an outflow of his character. That's a lot of words, let's narrow it down a bit. When the Bible uses *hesed*, it often elevates one characteristic in particular.

Hesed is about *loyalty*.

To be loyal is to be committed to someone regardless of how the relationship shifts in the future. This is because loyalty is an *outflow of character*, not a response to someone else. God has *hesed* like I have blue eyes. My eye color day to day does not depend on anyone or anything else. It just is. My wife is not loyal to me because my behavior causes her to be loyal. It's actually quite the opposite; she's still loyal to me *in spite* of my behavior. She demonstrates a version of *hesed* to me for no other reason than she chose to be my wife.

The *hesed* of God is not based on how we behave toward him. *God himself is loyally loving.* It's his character, not a response. God told Moses his name on that mountain, remember? God is all these things, all the time, because they make up who he is.

The Bible's emphasis on *hesed's* loyalty is seen nowhere as clearly as Psalm 136. Let's take 136:1 as an example (bracketed word added):

Give thanks to the Lord, for he is good!

His faithful love [hesed] *endures forever.*

David repeats this proclamation twenty-six times in the Psalm. The original Hebrew includes *hesed* but also the word for *forever* as well. So what David is trying to communicate is not so much the *intensity* of *hesed* but the *length*. What makes God's *hesed* love different from our love is it's loyal, enduring nature. God's love for us is a long love compared to our short bursts of love for him. Hear God's complaint in Hosea 6:4 (bracketed word added):

> *O Israel and Judah,*
> *what should I do with you?" asks the Lord.*
> *"For your love* [hesed] *vanishes like the morning mist*
> *and disappears like dew in the sunlight."*

What sets apart God's love is its permanency. Our love is like a mist, fragile and about to disappear. God's love sticks around. It's not affected by the temperature of the relationship. It's unfazed by seasons of drought.

God doesn't *do* love sometimes, he *is* love. And because he *is* love, he will never not be loving.

The Bible has a lot of things to say about *hesed,* but most of them have to do with its loyal endurance. There are two key reasons that God's love endures like a marathon runner while ours falls flat on its face like a baby taking their first steps. The loyal love of God *does not depend on God's feelings in the moment,* and *it is not affected by the response of the recipient.*

Here we are again in Hosea 11. Read verses 7-9:

> *For my people are determined to desert me.*
> *They call me the Most High,*
> *but they don't truly honor me.*
> *"Oh, how can I give you up, Israel?*
>
> *How can I let you go?*
> *How can I destroy you like Admah*
> *or demolish you like Zeboiim?*
> *My heart is torn within me,*
> *and my compassion overflows.*
>
> *No, I will not unleash my fierce anger.*
> *I will not completely destroy Israel,*
> *for I am God and not a mere mortal.*
> *I am the Holy One living among you,*
> *and I will not come to destroy.*

Notice at the end of this passage just how furious God was at the rebellion of his beloved people. He felt fierce anger with a desire to completely destroy everyone. He wanted to wipe the slate clean, to start over. It was that bad, and he was that angry.

Still, notice the sweet question in the section before. When people ask rhetorical questions like this, it's often to prove the point of impossibility. So God rhetorically asks, "How can I leave Israel?" He knows the answer. He can't. Leaving his people is an impossibility. God's *hesed* is not dependent on his feelings. *God can feel angry and still maintain hesed toward his people.*

In this passage, we also see how God's *hesed* is not dependent on how people respond to it. All God ever did to his people was show them covenant loyalty and in return, they abandoned him. We might even call God's love *wasted*. Look at how tenderly God showed his love to Israel as described in Hosea 11:1-4:

> *When Israel was a child, I loved him,*
> *and I called my son out of Egypt.*
>
> *But the more I called to him,*
> *the farther he moved from me,*
> *offering sacrifices to the images of Baal*
> *and burning incense to idols.*
>
> *I myself taught Israel how to walk,*
> *leading him along by the hand.*
> *But he doesn't know or even care*
> *that it was I who took care of him.*
>
> *I led Israel along*
> *with my ropes of kindness and love.*
> *I lifted the yoke from his neck,*
> *and I myself stooped to feed him.*

Can you hear the painful yearning in God's voice?

Some of you have experienced this. You know the heartbreak of a child's rejection. You know what it's like to raise your child, to wipe their toddler faces after a meal, to hold their soft hands as they learn to walk, to stand by them through the ups and downs of life only to be completely and utterly rejected as they grow up. All that time, energy, effort, love, and compassion just thrown away like it wasn't even there. It's gut-wrenching.

Maybe you've spent so much love on someone else, only to

have them walk away like it never even happened. You know that hollow feeling of rejection, too. Didn't your love mean anything to them?

This was God and us. Before we met Jesus, we were God's enemies (Romans 5:10). We were the child who enjoyed God's gracious blessings of life only to spit in his face and run away from home. Thanks for helping us grow up God, we got it from here.

The natural progression for all human parent/child relationships is for the child to eventually not need the parent anymore. This is a sign of maturity. With God however, the sign of maturity is not needing him less but *needing him more*. It's exactly the opposite. God has richly blessed us with everything we need. Even on those people who reject him, he gives the common graces of life, sunshine, fresh air, ocean waves, and starry nights. He is continually giving himself to all people, regardless of their response to him.

His continuous giving is meant to cause us to *want him more*. So when we take his gifts and run away, it's not only impolite; it's downright hateful. God wants to be wanted. He desires to be desired. God is glorified in our dependence on him.

God is good to all (Psalm 145:9), even as the response from much of his creation is rejection.

Weak, shallow forms of love would have given up, but God's loyal love sticks around even when we ignore it. God is determined to keep showering down love on his creatures who are determined to reject him. Here is Romans 5:6-8:

When we were utterly helpless, Christ came at just the right time and died for us sinners. Now, most people would not be willing to die for an upright person, though someone might perhaps be willing to die for a person who is especially good. But God showed his great love for us by sending Christ to die for us while we were still sinners.

Jesus didn't come to die for those who seemed like good people to die for. He didn't analyze the possibility of rejection or make judgments on dying for people who could provide the greatest potential to love him back. God sent Jesus to die for his enemies. God's *hesed* is for people who are vile, rebellious, and hostile. God keeps showing us loyal love because his choice to be committed to us isn't dependent on how we react to his gift. He is not discouraged by our lack of enthusiasm for his love. It keeps flowing upstream.

The story of the Bible is a story of *God showing loyal love to a people that don't want to love him back.* Time and time again, God moves in loving pursuit of a people who are not only indifferent to him, but openly hostile to him. We are not just neutral recipients of God's love. More often than not, in ways we regret to admit, we act in ways that are actively opposed to him. We reject his tender hand in favor of our own idols and vices, turning our noses up at the still, small voice of grace in favor of blatant sin and self-idolization.

We actively hurt the people we love. *God's hesed remains.*

We continually choose to love, serve, and obey our idols. *God's hesed remains.*

Hesed is undefinable. We don't have a concept of it. *It's too good.*

His enduring, loyal, loving pursuit of you is never stopping, never giving up, unbreaking, always and forever. His love is not just something he does. It's who he is.

God's eye color is loyal, committed, enduring love. Forget *The Notebook*, the story of Ruth drives this point home with even more force.

In the Old Testament, the book of Ruth is peculiar for a number of reasons. First, it breaks from the narrative-heavy theme of the Old Testament so far. The history, law, and war of the first seven books of the Old Testament give way to Ruth, a story about a single family living during the time of the Judges, as Israel was trying to get on its feet.

Unlike the majority of the Bible, Ruth doesn't place God at the center of the story. Sure, he is mentioned and heavily involved, but God is mostly *assumed* in the story of Ruth. No grand appearances. Read by itself, one might wonder why it's even in the Bible to begin with. What does this story have to do with anything?

The book of Ruth is about *hesed*.

Naomi is the first main character we meet in Ruth. She is wife to Elimelech and together they had two sons, Mahlon and Kilyon. This family was from Bethlehem but due to a famine they immigrated to Moab, a nation in conflict with Israel to the east.

Life was hard due to the famine, but it was even harder due to the fact that the family were refugees living among people who were sometimes hostile to Israelites. During their time in

Moab, Elimelech died, leaving Naomi widowed with her two sons. The sons married two Moabite women, Orpah and Ruth. The situation turned another horrific corner as Mahlon and Kilyon both die as well, leaving their mother Naomi suddenly childless, with her only surviving family members being the widows of her deceased sons.

The grieving Naomi had no reason to stay in Moab anymore, so she decided to head back to Israel and live among her people again. She begged Orpah and Ruth to stay in Moab with their own people and let her return to Israel by herself. She knew that Orpah and Ruth have absolutely no reason to stay with her, especially as they would be foreign widows in Israel. To be a Moabite widow living in Israel would automatically mean hostility and trouble, a hard life.

The women argue with Naomi a bit, but eventually Orpah agreed and returned to Moab. Ruth, on the other hand, refused to leave Naomi. She was married to her son, and that made them family. Ruth was committed to Naomi, no matter what the future brought. In Ruth 1:14-17, we read this exchange and Ruth's response to Naomi's insistence:

> And again they wept together, and Orpah kissed her mother-in-law good-bye. But Ruth clung tightly to Naomi. "Look," Naomi said to her, "your sister-in-law has gone back to her people and to her gods. You should do the same."
>
> But Ruth replied, "Don't ask me to leave you and turn back. Wherever you go, I will go; wherever you live, I will live. Your people will be my people, and your God will be my God. Wherever you die, I will die, and there I will

be buried. May the Lord punish me severely if I allow anything but death to separate us!"

If you look closely, you can see the *hesed* of Ruth. We see the women weeping together, a sign of deep distress. Ruth must have felt the weight of this moment, the intense anxiety that her situation brought on. *But even though Ruth was distressed, she committed to Naomi.* No matter how heavy and uncertain the future felt, she would not be scared off from staying with Naomi.

After Orpah leaves, Ruth stayed. Naomi saw what Ruth was trying to do, and she wouldn't have it. She'd already lost her husband and sons. She would not let her daughter-in-law willingly choose a life of hardship just because of her. As Ruth clung to her, Naomi pled again, "Ruth, don't do this. Don't follow me. I'm not worth it. Stay with your people, worship your god and forget about me."

Ruth heard the voice of her mother-in-law, and while good intentioned, it did nothing to change her mind. *Even as Naomi protested against her commitment, Ruth stayed.* Sure, if Ruth stayed in Moab, she probably would have been able to find a new husband and start a new family. Her life at least had a chance of redemption. But in this moment, looking into Naomi's eyes red with grief, Ruth declared her unwavering *hesed* to Naomi.

What people? *You are my people.* What God? *Your God is mine.*

So Ruth stayed with Naomi. Whatever the future holds, she would stay. Ruth was *bound* to Naomi.

I won't spoil the rest of the story, but you should really go ahead and read it sometime; it's beautiful. Ruth's *hesed* toward Naomi is rewarded and the whole story shifts from grief and despair to one of hope and redemption.

For us, this story is a rich illustration of *hesed*, with a special emphasis on its *binding nature*. Take another look at Ruth's response to Naomi. It almost feels like Ruth couldn't leave Naomi even if she tried. Ruth was not just trying to be courageous here. Through marriage to her son, Ruth was now committed to Naomi for life. In Ruth's mind, this was a cold, hard fact. This wasn't a spur-of-the-moment great idea on Ruth's part. Ruth's actions lined up with her identity as Naomi's daughter-in-law. As a relative to Naomi, she was bound to her.

This idea of being bound to someone else is central to our understanding of *hesed*. Like we've been saying, *hesed* flows out of God's identity. He can't not demonstrate *hesed*.

If you were to survey the Bible and discover the most popular metaphors God uses to describe his relationship with his people, you'd probably discover God as Father to be the most popular. But there is another metaphor God routinely uses to help explain just how committed he is to his children: the metaphor of *marriage*.

There's not a whole lot of difference between what God is trying to get across when he uses these two metaphors. Both seem to indicate love, compassion, and loyalty. But there is, at least to me, one major difference between the two: choice.

You don't really get to pick your kid. I'm not getting into *how* they are created right now, but they definitely are not put together by you. You don't get to choose which parts of your personality are included, if they are introverted or extroverted, or whether or not they will have two completely different shaped ears like me.

It's different with marriage. In the biblical context, husbands were able to choose who they committed themselves to. Today, in most parts of the world, marriage is a choice from both individuals. You get to know their good and bad sides, and after a period of relationship, you vow to commit yourself to them forever.

This is why I think God was on to something when he made the choice to explain himself like a husband to his wife. Like a husband, God knew what he was getting into. He knew we would be inconsistent lovers of him. He knew about our hard-to-shake vices that rob us of relationship. Yet none of that really matters in the end, because like a husband to his wife, God has chosen to be *bound* to us. Listen to this metaphor of marriage used beautifully in Hosea 2:19-20:

> *I will make you my wife forever,*
> *showing you righteousness and justice,*
> *unfailing love and compassion.*
>
> *I will be faithful to you and make you mine,*
> *and you will finally know me as the Lord.*

God has chosen you. Has your heart forgotten that? Moment after moment, day after day, through valleys and mountains, sunshine and rain. The creator of the universe has made a choice to bind you to himself. Because of that incredible fact, God's default attitude toward you is that of a faithful husband. Out of his identity as a husband to his people, flows righteousness, justice, love and compassion. *The foundation for the hesed of God is the reality that he has bound himself to us like a faithful husband to his wife.* This is why God is able to continue to show us loyal, steadfast love even when he doesn't feel like it, and even when we reject it.

A faithful husband doesn't care if he *feels* like loving his wife; he is bound to her, so he just does it.

A faithful husband doesn't care if his wife *rejects or ignores* his attempts at love. He is bound to her, so he still shows it.

The prophet Jeremiah says it this way:

> *I have loved you with an everlasting love; therefore I have continued my faithfulness* [hesed] *to you.* (Jeremiah 31:3b ESV, bracketed word added)

Not because we can pay him back, not because we always love him in return, not because he saw the potential of our future self, and not because we'll be the spouse he deserves in return, *but because God loved us, he will continue to love us.*

He loved you yesterday, so he'll love you today.

And because he loves you today, he'll love you tomorrow.

If you're feeling a little confused here, it's because this line of thinking is known as circular reasoning, and it would be a logical fallacy except for the fact that God's *hesed* is meant to defy logic. It's too wonderful to make sense; it's too big to fit logically in our minds.

We can only hope that with time, we'll get a better awareness of the width, length, height, and depth of God's *hesed* for us. God has given us his people as the means of bringing us just a little bit closer to the reality of this logic-defying love.

I'm currently sitting at my kitchen table with a nice, velvety Bordeaux and thinking to myself, "How on earth am I supposed to suggest that we imitate the *hesed* of God in our own church communities? Isn't that, like, impossible?"

Impossible yes, but does that mean we should just give up? Not at all. We're disciples of Jesus, you betcha.

We're going to continue rolling with this idea of *hesed as being bound to someone else,* but this time, we are going to apply it to living in the family of God. Please, turn in your Bibles to Romans 12, or just read verses 3-5 below:

> *Because of the privilege and authority God has given me, I give each of you this warning: Don't think you are better than you really are. Be honest in your evaluation of yourselves, measuring yourselves by the faith God has given us. Just as our bodies have many parts and each part has a special function, so it is with Christ's body. We are many parts of one body, and we all belong to each other.*

Paul has just instructed the Romans to give their whole selves to God. True worship is not singing one fast, one medium, and two slow songs on a Sunday morning and calling it good. The kind of worship God accepts is a gritty, sacrificial, whole-life type of worship.

Keeping with this theme of true worship, Paul then defines what true community is like. The thrust of his message comes in his comparing the family of God to a connected, interdependent body. This is the truest reality of the church: *we are bound to each other.*

If you were to randomly pick five church websites to investigate, chances are you would find some language on them about living like family. Apparently, every church in America lives like family according to their website. While this is a great goal and a good tagline for a website, I would be willing to bet that the actual reality of community life differs from the goals listed on the "Who We Are" section of the webpage.

In American culture, freedom is prized above all things. Because the American church is in America (such an enlightened thought, right?), the church itself is susceptible to this over-prioritization of individual freedom as well. With regards to joining and being a part of a church, we are free to come, free to go, free to do anything we want. As a result, there is a tendency for us who call the American church home to base our commitment to a group of people on our lived experience with them. If we continue to have positive experiences with the church we are a part of, we will continue to commit to them. If our experiences suddenly turn negative, shifting our commitment to a new community seems more attractive. We are free to do whatever we want, no questions asked.

Shallow communities tend to prioritize personal experience over commitment.

Hesed communities prioritize commitment that transcends personal experience.

When conflict arises in a shallow community, the first thought is to *run from each other.*

When conflict arises in a *hesed* community, the first thought is to *fight for each other.*

In a shallow setting, people are bound to each other based on experience. In a family with *hesed* at the center, people experience each other based on the fact that they are already bound to one another. It's this simple change of priority that separates a relationship of *hesed* from everything else.

When you get hired as an airline pilot, there's about two months of training to be completed before you get to fly the real jet. During this time of training, you get paired up with a partner who will go through all the lessons together, learning alongside you as you both work toward the goal of completing training.

During training at the airline I was hired at, I was assigned a training partner. At first, things were going well, but as the simulator lessons got more challenging, my partner started to fall behind. I was on track, but our training schedule was delayed because of her struggles. One day, after a particularly grueling training session, I found her outside the training building, sitting down on the curb, with her head in her hands, trying to hold back tears. She was defeated and ashamed that she was holding our schedule back with her need to repeat lessons and since I was her partner, I was held back too.

I told her that either we were going to complete our training together or we weren't going to complete it at all. Because I was her partner, I wasn't going to leave if things got hard. We both had a common goal (to be an airline pilot), and I had made a commitment to getting our training done, together.

The next day, the director of training approached me and asked if I wanted to separate from my training partner and finish up the course on my own. I'd be able to move at my own pace again without my partner delaying my progress. I respectfully declined. I don't know what it was about that situation, but I had a feeling in my heart that I couldn't abandon my partner; we needed to finish together.

After a few more lessons, things started to click, and we finished our new-hire training together. We were delayed in being able to finish, but that didn't matter much in the end. I made a decision to stick with her because of my prior commitment, no matter how things turned out. Commitment preceding and in spite of experience. This is *hesed.*

As we've been discussing, the foundational reality that drives the *hesed* of God is that of God being bound to us. Because God believes that he is bound to us, he is able to show us incredibly loyal love, no matter how he is feeling in the moment and no matter how we choose to respond. As we devote ourselves to the family of God, our *dedication to relationally pursue one another* is the bridge we can use to more fully understand and experience the *hesed* of God.

For many of us, the steadfast love of God has remained stuck as a theological concept in our minds because we have little to no experience being loyally loved by another person. Human love is cheap, inconsistent, and fleeting. We've all had experiences of seasons of closeness with another person only to have that love fade away with time.

To be people who cultivate *hesed,* we must take the responsibility upon ourselves to continually pursue other followers of Jesus on a regular basis, no matter the season of life.

It's more than just meeting with your small group once a week. I suggest you identify one to five people in your life that you'll commit to pursuing at the highest level of all relationships you currently have. These people will be put at the top of your relational list. They will get the first of your time, emotional energy, and prayer. Commit to them first and deal with the results later. We are using the model given to us by Jesus. He had twelve disciples, but he chose three as his closest friends. Go and do likewise.

There are over fifty "one-anothers" in the Bible. If you call yourself a member of God's family, you are commanded by Scripture to do things like love, teach, build up, forgive, be patient with, speak the truth in love, submit to, comfort, show hospitality toward, and confess sins to one another.

And here's my personal favorite: singing to one another (Ephesians 5:16). When's the last time you and your friend, spouse, roommate, or neighbor just sang a song of worship together? (What? That would be too awkward?)

What's really awkward is thinking you're an active member of the body of Christ and realizing that you actually aren't. The one-anothers of Scripture are commands. By committing to practicing these commands regularly with a few friends, you'll get a tangible experience of what the *hesed* of God is like.

I don't want you to miss this. Think about the friends you love the most. They all struggle sometimes with accepting the *hesed* of God. Could the reason for their doubt of God's love for them not be so much a result of their weak faith, but the fact that *you have failed to love them* in a way that shows them what God's love is like? Could *your* lack of constant pursuit of them be the reason they fail to believe in a God who loves them without restraint? Just sit with that for a moment. God will often use the animating presence of the Holy Spirit in someone to call someone else to himself. We should work to allow the Holy Spirit access to ourselves for his purposes. Oftentimes, we are the answers to our prayers for others.

I want to finish out this chapter with Galatians 3:26-28:

> *For you are all children of God through faith in Christ Jesus. And all who have been united with Christ in baptism have put on Christ, like putting on new clothes. There is no longer Jew or Gentile, slave or free, male and female. For you are all one in Christ Jesus.*

In God's family, the lines that we use to categorize people are still there, but they don't matter. There are rich and poor people in God's family, but how much money you have doesn't matter. There are people of different ethnic backgrounds in God's family, but no ethnicity is better than the other. God's family is made up of men and women. Both are equally valuable and honored in the family of God.

Where our pursuit of others really shines is when we focus our energy toward others who don't look like us, act like us, or come from our same background. This is where our attempts to imitate the *hesed* of God can be a testimony to the world of God's wide, unifying love.

Every summer, our house churches take a picture during a camp retreat. I love looking at all the different types of people we have, from all different types of backgrounds. If you were to look at that picture, you might wonder what in the world all these different people were doing together. On some level, they don't seem to belong.

That's what the *hesed* of God does. When we bind ourselves to the family of God, we don't get to pick the types of people we bind ourselves with. God chooses who makes up his family, and we must bind ourselves with whomever he chooses. Differences cause misunderstanding. Different family backgrounds can cause conflict. But the *hesed* of God transcends all that. By committing to pursue one another with a love that isn't affected by how we feel or by the reaction of the recipient, we give one another a small taste of the *hesed* of God.

Be the one who shows someone else what the loyal love of God is like.

In an act of *hesed*, the son of God let people that were made in his image nail his hands and feet to a wooden cross. He was bound to that cross for us.

As Jesus hung on that cross as a public spectacle, the insults started raining down. In Matthew 27:39-44 we read of the sarcastic jeers the crowd mercilessly shouted at him as he hung naked and beaten beyond recognition on the cross. They reminded Jesus that he once said he could rebuild the entire temple in three days, so breaking free from the cross shouldn't be that difficult. The religious leaders even joined in, begging this all-powerful, divinely-appointed homeless rabbi to prove his authority by asking God to rescue him. It got so bad that even the half-dead criminals who were going through their own crucifixions next to Jesus started to taunt and ridicule him in between their last gasps of breath. Everyone wanted Jesus to back up what he said.

What's amazing here is that *Jesus could have come down*. He was God, complete with all the power that created and sustained the world. He had millions of angels at his beck and call, ready to obey him at a moment's notice. It was entirely within Jesus' ability to come off that cross and show everyone his power.

But he didn't. Jesus chose to remain bound to the cross. Why?

Because Jesus is bound to you.

The reason the *hesed* of God rests on you, right now, is because Jesus didn't come down off that cross. Imagine the weak, quivering voice of Christ as he asked where his father was (Mt. 27:46).

Jesus felt distressed, but his *hesed* remained.

Picture Jesus receiving the mockery of the crowds. Hear the sneering, sarcastic voices raining down on the beaten Son of God. Jesus was going through this horrific act of love *for them*.

The crowds sarcastically rejected Jesus' great act of love, but his *hesed* remained.

I'm not sure how long you have been following Jesus. Maybe it's been for a long time, or maybe not. Maybe you've never even thought about devoting your life to him. I do know that your sin has caused God great grief and anger.

Even as you have grieved and angered your heavenly Father by your willful disobedience, his *hesed* is for you, this very moment.

I also know that there have been many times in life where God has richly blessed you. He's provided for you when you needed provision, he has loved you when you needed love. But even as God has demonstrated his great love toward you, it has often been met with rejection. You have been offered the grace of God only to decide to reject it in favor of your own desires.

Even as you have rejected his love, Jesus offers you his *hesed*, right now. Even as you lay unresponsive in that hospital bed, unable to remember, Jesus just keeps showing up. He is committed to you, even when you aren't fully committed to him.

God has been showing up in your life since the second you were born. Like Allie from *The Notebook,* we are all suffering with this spiritual form of dementia, that causes us to not recognize Jesus who sits beside our hospital bed, reading to us of his love and commitment to us. Day after day he reads to us and day after day we just sit there, unresponsive. Our sinfulness causes us to forget all that he has done for us, all the hidden ways he has shown up during our stay on earth. We are so busy living, so busy forgetting. In spite of our forgetfulness, he comes back the next morning and does it all over again, reading to us, calling to us, waiting for us to wake up and respond to his offering of loyal love.

Let this be the morning of your new life. Let this moment, wherever you are right now, be the moment you wake up and remember. He has always been there. Don't you see it? All the tender mercies you have experienced in your life was his voice gently calling out to you. In all the deep pain, he was there sitting, waiting, hoping with you.

In my experience, when Jesus shows up, it's not in a powerful, abstract way. There aren't many burning bushes anymore. I have found that the way Jesus most often shows up to humans like you and me is through other people bringing his actual presence into our lives. Jesus dwells in and among his people, so it only makes sense that his power and presence would be mediated through his people as well.

Jesus wants to bring his *hesed* to earth through the *hesed* of his people. He is looking for people to partner with him in the renewal of all things, and you are the exact person He's looking for. We have an amazing opportunity to show the world just how loyally God loves them by practicing the *hesed* of God with one another.

Together, we can unbind the powers of evil in our own hearts and in the world by choosing to bind ourselves to one another with the *hesed* of Christ.

CHAPTER 10

SUNSHINE

OUR HOUSE WAS built in 1916. Thankfully, much of the old house feel has been preserved throughout the years by the various owners, so it still carries that old home charm. The hardwood floors are original, as well as most of the leaded windows. We have a gorgeous hand-plastered ceiling in our living room, and the basement even has a small door which was used for coal delivery back in the day. It is a stately and incredibly drafty house to live in.

One of the most beautiful features of our home is the built-in buffet in our dining room. It's such a majestic piece that we use some of it to store our nice dishes and glassware. The other drawers are used for something else every parent does battle with on a semi-regular basis: kid art supplies.

Yes, I am sorry to say that our gorgeous, history-laden, hand-crafted buffet has been relegated as the keeper of crayons, construction paper, and glue. And as the holder of art supplies, our kids regularly rip through the cabinets with an alarming rate of speed, pulling open drawers and searching for various mediums with which to express their creativity.

As a result, our buffet is regularly in shambles, which frustrates my wife and me to no end. It's a shame to see such a thoughtfully crafted piece of furniture treated so harshly, but kids will be kids, I guess.

One evening, I was driving home from work. It was one of those days where my anger was like a pile of dry, dead wood, just waiting for a spark to set it ablaze. I arrived home and proceeded to put my backpack in the dining room when I saw the spark I so desperately desired: the drawers of the buffet were all opened with paper, markers, stickers, and yarn pouring out from every which way. My son was at the dining room table, surrounded by piles of art supplies, feverishly working on some sort of picture.

I lost it.

Before even saying hello to my boy, I raised my voice at him, scolding and shaming, and sent him upstairs. As the dust of my temper tantrum settled, I felt this sinking feeling form in the pit of my stomach:

Oh no. What did I just do? That's not me. What just happened is not who Matt is.

My behavior in that moment had strayed so far from who I was and who I wanted to be. I felt the heavy weight of shame and regret. There was a deep sense of disconnect inside me—I acted like a completely different person, a total stranger to myself.

In a moment of weakness, my actions did not line up with who I knew I was.

As followers of Jesus, we know who we are. We know how we are to act. We've read all the verses and listened to all the sermons. The fruits of the Spirit have been memorized and memorialized on our Instagram. *Be holy, for I am holy.* Yeah God, we get it.

But there's a fight going on inside all of us, between the Spirit of God and our sin-infested flesh. Some days, like me with my artist son, the work of God's spirit in our lives is completely eclipsed by our sin-nature. As a result, our "living by the Spirit" is incredibly inconsistent. We often don't live or love like Jesus. The reality is that we have the power of the Holy Spirit inside us, but our actions say otherwise. Our behavior is inconsistent.

This inconsistency is not just a problem for us to wrestle with internally. Our inconsistency to match our lives with our love for Jesus hurts other people. You should have seen the look on my son's face when I lashed out at him. His pencil fell out of his hand, his lips neutralized into a straight, emotionless line, and his eyes got big, watery, and empty. The worst part of it all was when I found out what he was working on:

It was a picture of him and I holding our little stick hands, with the words "I love daddy" written with all the sincerity a five-year-old could muster.

I am an inconsistent lover of Jesus. My actions do not always line up with my beliefs. I will often say one thing, preach one thing, counsel someone else with one thing, and do another.

If my life is a play, my role is a follower of Jesus, and I often act out of character.

God is not like that. He always acts rightly. He is always consistent. He never acts out of character.

God is truth, and he is always true to himself.

In other words, God is *faithful*.

And like we have been discovering, God doesn't just choose to be faithful; his very identity is faithfulness. It's so ingrained in God's identity that even God's actual name reflects faithfulness. When Moses asked God's name in Exodus 3, God answered him. God called himself *faithfulness*.

Moses was a Hebrew born in Egypt. Shortly after his birth, the decree to kill all Hebrew baby boys was issued by Pharaoh to slow the growth of the Hebrew population in Egypt. Moses' mother hid him from the Egyptians until he was three months old, and then she came up with a plan to save her little boy's life: she would place him in a basket and float him down the Nile River toward the palace of Pharaoh where he would hopefully be rescued by a merciful Egyptian woman—a last-ditch effort by a desperate mother trying to save her son's life.

The plan worked. Moses was discovered by the daughter of Pharaoh who raised him as an Egyptian. Due to his status as a member of Pharaoh's family, Moses grew in power and influence within the Egyptian government, all the while being a Hebrew. This all came to a grinding halt one day when Moses ended up killing an Egyptian who was beating a Hebrew slave.

Fearing for his life, Moses decided to run away from Egypt and settled in the land of Midian, just to the east.

Years passed. One day, Moses was herding sheep in the wilderness when a strange sight caught his eye. A bush was on fire, yet it wasn't burning up. Moses approached the bush and the voice of God called out to him. God announced to Moses his grand plan to free his people from the grip of the Egyptians and that Moses was the man for the job. Moses needed to tell the Israelite slaves about the God that sent him. Even *Moses* wasn't sure who this God was yet. So Moses asked for God's name. How about something powerful, something commanding, something that will inspire confidence in the hearts of the fearful, oppressed Hebrews in Egypt?

YHWH acquiesces to Moses' request and tells him his name: *I am who I am.*

Or just "I am" for short.

I am. That's it. That's the name of the supreme ruler of the universe. I would love to know what was running through Moses' mind after that grand announcement.

While simple, this name is an incredibly loaded declarative statement, and to understand it fully, we need to know two things about the religious landscape of Moses' time.

First, there were a lot of gods out there. In Egypt alone, more than two thousand different deities were recognized. That's a lot of different gods to know and worship. This plethora of options for god-worship wasn't just restricted to Egypt though. The entire world was flooded with a countless number of divine beings who required worship. The world back then was more *enchanted,* remember?

Second, the gods back then were incredibly unstable. They often didn't act according to character. This is why so much of the sacrifice and worship back then was to "appease" them. The gods were often angry or about to get angry, so you better worship them or else. They weren't worshiped for their holiness primarily; they were worshiped so you wouldn't experience their wrath. Their actions rose and fell with their emotions, and it was a wild ride.

God calling himself *I am who I am* takes these cultural assumptions head on.

First, he is the only true God. his name is the ultimate statement of self-sufficiency. He is the uncreated one, eternally existing. He is not a figment of your imagination. He always was, always is, and always will be. He is *the* God among gods.

Second, he is *eternally consistent.* Another way we can translate God's name here is *whatever I am, I will always be.* Compared to the emotionally insecure and unstable gods of Moses' day, he is the picture of rock-solid stability. his actions always flow out of his character. his character doesn't change over time; he is the same God yesterday, today, and forever. his actions are always consistent.

I am who I am is a statement of God's faithfulness.

The reason God is so faithful to *us* is that he is so faithful to *himself.* This is the big idea for this chapter. God loves himself and his name. He has an untamed passion for who he is, and he is extremely concerned with his name being worshiped. This isn't selfish on God's part. In fact, God's devotion to himself is our greatest good. Discussing God's faithfulness is great and all, but like eating a pizza with bacon and pineapple over and over again, it gets old after a while.

God's *faithfulness* is one of those attributes that, due to chronic overuse, has become watered down in many minds and hearts of Christians. It seems like you can't get through a Sunday morning without mentioning the faithfulness of God. This is a good thing, if we are talking about *faithfulness* the way God wants us to understand it.

The classic church-going American definition for God's faithfulness is something about his continual provision for us. When we sing of his faithfulness, we're often picturing times in our minds when God has provided for *our* needs, or shown up in ways we didn't expect. To trust in God's faithfulness usually means believing that he will provide for some specific need or desire in the future. In this definition of faithfulness, God is viewed more like the United States Postal Service—sometimes late but always delivering.

If this is where your mind goes when it thinks about God's faithfulness, there's no shame from me, it's certainly a big part of mine. The thing is, God's works *are* to be remembered. There's so much in the Bible about remembering the works of God and recounting his faithful deeds. He *has* been faithful to us in the past, he *is* faithful to us now, and he will *continue* to be faithful to us in the future.

Amen and hallelujah.

Here's the problem though. Think back to Adam and Eve with the tree that was off limits in the garden. Do you remember how Satan tempted Eve to eat the fruit off that tree? He told her that God was keeping a secret from her. Satan claimed that if she ate the fruit off the tree, she would become like God.

Eve was tempted with the possibility of becoming like God, and this temptation has been at the root of the fall of humanity ever since.

We want to be the focal point of the universe. That's our hearts' greatest longing. This desire manifests itself in a million different ways, but the root is still there. Selfishness, pride, jealousy—it's all rooted in this backwards self-centeredness that's woven into the fiber of our being.

And because we're self-centered by default, our view of God's faithfulness suffers. *Our understanding of God's faithfulness is distorted by our inherent desire to view ourselves as the center of our reality.* This is why when most of us think about God being faithful, we think of the ways he has provided *for us* in our times of need. In our minds, God is faithful because he always provides what *we* need. By default, we make God's faithfulness about us.

While that definition is certainly *a part* of God's faithfulness, I would like to argue that it's a subpart under a much truer and glorious vision: God's attribute of faithfulness means that *God is always true to himself and to his character.* He always acts in line with who he is. He never does anything that disagrees with his character. It's no wonder that the Hebrew word for *faithfulness* in Exodus 34:6 is *emeth,* which means truth, reliability, and firmness. God's faithfulness is less about us and our experiences, and more about God and his consistent nature.

This is the reason I think God saved faithfulness for last in Exodus 34. God's faithfulness is why the other four attributes can exist. It's his faithfulness that is the foundation for our ability to trust in his compassion, grace, slowness of anger, and loyal love. When God calls himself faithful, we can trust that:

God is compassionate *all the time*

God is gracious *all the time*

God is slow to anger *all the time*

God is loyally loving *all the time*

God's faithfulness is the glue that holds all of his character together. It's what differentiates his character from ours. It's what makes him a better God than the idols we continually run to. It's why he is worthy of worship.

God's faithfulness is like the tendons and ligaments that connect our muscles and bones together. Without those, we'd just be a lifeless mass, unable to move. Muscles are great, bones are necessary, but they're totally useless unless they are connected to the body as a whole. Our ligaments and tendons are what gives our bodies shape, form, and the ability to move. God's faithfulness allows us to believe in a God with structure, with truth, with consistency. Faithfulness makes God *dependable*.

If God was gracious only when he felt like it, that wouldn't be very praiseworthy, would it? If he was slow to anger only when you caught him in a good mood, could he really call himself slow to anger? No. God's faithfulness assures us that all his other qualities continue forever. If all of God's attributes are a thanksgiving feast, his faithfulness is the salt that makes everything else better.

Before God is faithful to *us*, he is faithful to *himself.*

And that is really, really good news.

When we do what we say, when our actions line up with our words, that is a way we love others. I was not consistent, not faithful to my son that afternoon. He was hurt by my failure to act according to the truths that I believed about myself. Unfortunately, many of us have experienced harm from inconsistent people, or even worse, we have been the inconsistent person to hurt someone else.

Humans are incredibly complex, and the reasons for our actions are often illogical and inconsistent. At the most basic level, much of our actions are driven by our basic needs to feel loved, respected, and accepted or to push away feelings of guilt, shame, or fear. We are irrational creatures, marked by erratic actions that don't often make much sense. We are driven by the winds of our emotions, unable to rise above our situations and see things clearly for what they are.

God is not like that. When God acts, he acts with purpose and clear, unadulterated motivation. The Bible is unanimous on what drives God to act the way he does. All of God's feelings and actions find their source in one specific cause.

When God feels, thinks, or acts, he does so *for the sake of his name.*

This concept of God acting for the sake of his name is all over Scripture. From Moses to David, and into the New Testament, it's clear that God's main driving motivation for doing what he does is a concern for his name. If I included just a sample of the instances where the sake of God's name is included, this chapter would be incredibly long, and I'd probably lose you. So let's take a look at one passage from the book of Ezekiel. Chapter 20 of the book of Ezekiel is a retelling of the history between God and his people. In short, God is continually pursuing his people in love only to have them reject him time and time again. This continual rejection would be enough to make anyone's faithfulness evaporate, but not the God of Israel. Three times in Ezekiel 20 we see the reason God maintained his commitment to his people even when they left him. Here is Ezekiel 20:8-9 (emphasis added) for reference:

> *But they rebelled against me and would not listen. They did not get rid of the vile images they were obsessed with, or forsake the idols of Egypt. Then I threatened to pour out my fury on them to satisfy my anger while they were still in Egypt. But I didn't do it, for **I acted to protect the honor of my name**. I would not allow shame to be brought on my name among the surrounding nations who saw me reveal myself by bringing the Israelites out of Egypt.*

Verses 13-14 and 21-22 of Ezekiel 20 follow the same line of reasoning. The people of God resisted and disobeyed him, God got angry but ultimately chose not to punish his people out of anger, all for the *sake of his name*.

Take a breath here because what I'm about to explain is extremely important to understand. We are getting a peek behind God's motivation for honoring his name above all things. God isn't being faithful because his people deserve it. He isn't even being faithful because He's obligated to. No, the reason God is continuing in faithfulness to his people is to preserve the honor and dignity of his name *in the sight of all the other, evil, unbelieving nations.*

Israel was a small country surrounded by large, powerful nations who were looking for an opportunity to strike. These other nations had heard about the God of Israel and how he would always protect them. God made a covenant promise to his people to be their protector. So, if he were to break that promise, then what would the other nations think? If God were to one day decide to become unfaithful and leave his people, his name would be the laughingstock of the world. The God of Israel would have been relegated to the thousands of other weak, false gods who have littered the minds and hearts of people since the beginning of time. If God were to stop being faithful, he would become irrelevant in the eyes of the world.

God will not let that happen. He will not give the nations of the world any reason to believe he's not faithful. God is too passionate about the honor of his name. He is too concerned with his name being synonymous with faithfulness to let it be disrespected.

And for us today, this is where it gets really good.

God loves himself. He loves his name. He desires the whole wide world to know, honor, and worship his name. This is God's highest desire: the glorification of his name. These two desires of God—his passion for his name and his faithfulness to you—are one in the same. They are two cords of the same rope.

Because God desires to glorify his name, he will continue being faithful to you.

And as God continues to be faithful to you, his name will be glorified.

If God were to suddenly stop being faithful to you, his name would suffer dishonor. And God does not tolerate dishonor to his name.

So from God's point of view, there's no reason to panic, no reason to whip yourself up in a frenzy of working to stay in God's good graces. God is at peace with you (Romans 5:1). Our desires to make ourselves lovely, acceptable, or worthy of relationship with God come from the doubts that Satan puts into our minds. Satan's weapon of choice is guilt, and he wields it skillfully.

And what's interesting is that his accusations are *actually true.* We *don't* deserve the love of God. We are *not* good enough. Our sins *really do* separate us from God. He's got a point, and we would be guilty before God *if* God's faithfulness toward us was about *our* behavior and *our* holiness and *our* obedience.

But it's not.

I wish you were sitting across from me in this coffee shop I'm in today. I would put my hands on your shoulders, look right into your eyes, and say this:

Friend, God's faithfulness *to you* has never been *about you.*

God promised that no matter how bad it looks, no matter how far you've strayed, and no matter how estranged you get, he will never stop honoring his name. In God's mind, his name is honored when he continues to show you faithfulness. So God, in his effort to protect the holiness, majesty, and glory of his own name, will never stop maintaining faithfulness to you. He will not give Satan any reason to think that he's won. There is a direct line between God's forgiveness and his faithfulness to his name as seen in 1 John 2:12 (ESV):

> *I am writing to you, little children, because your sins are forgiven for his name's sake.*

It's out of a concern for his name that God forgives you. God continually forgives because he is continually doing what's best for the honor of his name. Forgiveness is a miracle between God and himself. The forgiveness you receive from God is the byproduct of the passion he has for himself. God's love for you is a result of his love for himself and his name. This doesn't release us from the responsibility we have to repent and turn away from our sin, but the forgiveness we receive that makes repentance possible was a commitment God made to stay true to himself. Because of God's faithfulness, we don't have to wonder if our repentance will be accepted by God. It always will because he is always the same.

Satan has a popular lie he comes back to often, and it goes something like this: God loved you a lot when you first placed your faith in him, but over time, as you kept messing up, God has grown increasingly frustrated with you. You feel that? Think back to when you first trusted Jesus. At that moment, God's forgiveness was yours. All God's affections were kindled toward you. his compassion, grace, slowness of anger, and loyal love were all yours in infinite supply.

But life is hard. We are broken. What began as sweet, blissful love has morphed into something hard, frustrating, and cold.

Here's the beautiful truth: *God's attitude toward you at that very first moment of faith is his exact same attitude toward you right now.* How?

I am who I am.

God is the same today as he was yesterday.

God will be the same tomorrow as he is today.

Many of us view God's faithfulness like the water at the bottom of a deep well. We have to do the work of lowering the bucket, filling it with water, and pulling it up to receive it. Over time, the well has been getting deeper and deeper. God must need more effort from me as this relationship goes on, right? We feel this need to put on our best behavior in order to deserve the water. We need to prove that we deserve the water of God's faithfulness by being good enough people. Our works determine our worth.

God's faithfulness is nothing like that. His faithfulness to you is a *waterfall*, a constant rush of fresh grace, new mercy, renewed faithfulness. In a waterfall, there is never "old" water. It's always new. With his faithfulness, there is no striving to keep up your end of a bargain.

So stop looking down that deep, dark well. Put down your bucket and let go of the rope.

Place your heart under the torrential downpour that is his faithfulness *and just receive it.*

> *Yet I call this to mind,*
>
> *and therefore I have hope:*
>
> *Because of the Lord's faithful love*
>
> *we do not perish,*
>
> *for his mercies never end.*
>
> *They are new every morning;*
>
> *great is your faithfulness!*
>
> (Lamentations 3:21-23 CSB)

∽

It's one thing to *understand* God's faithfulness. It's quite another to *experience* it.

That's where the family of God comes in. By devoting ourselves to the family of God, we have the opportunity to experience faithfulness from one another on a micro level that mirrors the faithfulness that God shows us on a macro level.

But the way this happens might be a bit surprising.

Remember, the first thing we need to know about God's faithfulness is that it's directed at God himself first, then to us. God is faithful to us because he is first faithful to himself. In the family of God, this is no different.

With God, we indirectly receive the benefits of his faithfulness to himself. Likewise in the family of God, other people indirectly receive the benefits of our personal faithfulness to God.

This is how we can mirror God's faithfulness in the family of God.

The starting point for us to experience God's faithfulness in the family of God is to direct our individual faithfulness to God first, and then to each other. Committing ourselves as individuals to faithfully following Jesus does two things: we become a blessing for the flourishing of the Church, and we become people worthy of imitation for the growth of the church.

I have no hesitation claiming devotion to my wife over my children. I try my hardest (and fail often) to put her needs over my kids. While this may raise a few eyebrows, I have a reason for this order: The welfare and flourishing of my children is directly related to how much (or how little) I devote myself to my wife first. If we are in harmony, our children will benefit. If we are in strife, they will suffer.

Every day, we are bombarded with things that compete for our love and attention. What you and I need to figure out is how to be faithful to the *right things in the right order.* And if you call yourself a follower of Jesus, he makes it clear who should be on top in Matthew 6:33:

> *Seek the Kingdom of God above all else, and live righteously, and he will give you everything you need.*

Our lives should be marked by a relentless pursuit of God. This is the starting point for everything else. The mature follower of Jesus has the ability to rightly order their faithfulness to place

God and his Kingdom at the center of their existence. Above family, above work, above friends. This is how it's supposed to go. If we do that, Jesus promises us that everything we need will come in its own time.

Want a better marriage? Need more job satisfaction? Not content with how many digits are in your checking account? For all these "needs," start with a relentless, whole-hearted pursuit of Jesus.

(And spoiler alert, his solution to your money problems will probably not be addressed by adding more zeros to your bank account...)

This might come off as a little harsh, but if you want to show people true faithfulness, you need to put them in the back seat to your relationship to Christ. This is how God orders his faithfulness, first to himself and then to us. In the family of God, it should be no different. What the person sitting next to you at church needs more than anything else is *for you to be like Jesus*. You can't become like Jesus without walking with him regularly.

Your faithful pursuit of Jesus is a gift to those around you. The close relationship you experience with Christ directly impacts every single person in your path—from your spouse and children to your friends at church to the person ringing up your groceries who is having trouble finding the code for those organic bananas.

As we prioritize faithfulness to Jesus above each other, we will become more like him. This is what the people around us need the most: *for us to act like Jesus*. The fruits of the Spirit are a good place to start in this endeavor. In Galatians 5:22-23, Paul lists nine "results" of the Holy Spirit working in our lives. These are love, joy, peace, patience, kindness, goodness, faithfulness, and self-control.

I'm willing to bet many of us know people personally who embody these characteristics in greater measure than most. When you're around that person, you can't help but feel this invisible force drawing you into greater devotion to Christ. It seems like when that person enters the room, the Spirit of Jesus is there and that's because, well, he is.

So the emphasis on "God first" in our order of faithfulness is not at the expense of the people we love. We place God first *in order to be people of love.* The people in your life don't need your hot theological takes, or your armchair advice. They need one thing from you: to devote your life to the relentless pursuit of the person of Jesus, and to be transformed by your faithfulness to him.

As we become like him, this has an effect on the people around us. You'll walk around this world with the aroma of Christ, and to the people around you who are trying to follow Jesus, this will be a sweet, encouraging aroma. Just being with Jesus provides benefits for the people around you. But there's more. Your pursuit of Jesus will cause you to be a *person worth imitating,* and this is the design for how the church is to grow in maturity. This is Paul speaking in 1 Corinthians 11:1:

> You should imitate me, just as I imitate Christ.

Kind of a bold statement from Paul here. What's interesting is that he just got done talking about the freedom we have in Jesus to differ in opinion and action on various non-essential things like eating and drinking. He ends his "everyone can decide for themselves" message with a statement that essentially commands people to copy the way he follows Jesus. What gives, Paul?

We all need people in our lives that provide real-world examples of how to faithfully follow Jesus in our time and cultural moment. It is one thing to know in our heads that we should love our enemies, but it's quite another to hear from a friend how they are navigating loving their neighbors who run a crack house next door that gets shot up regularly. True story.

People need you to show them by your life what it looks like to faithfully follow Jesus in your specific context. They need you to be an example to copy.

How does someone follow Jesus in the twenty-first century with bills to pay, laundry to do, kids to feed, jobs to maintain, cars to repair, vacations to go on, and budgets to balance? What does seeking God's kingdom first look like in a world that seems to be constantly teetering on the edge of destruction? How do I actually be a Christian in my specific, unique life?

I love good sermons. I love thought-provoking podcasts. I love theological discussions about abstract ideas. Okay, that last one was a lie. Those modes of teaching fall short with regards to helping people apply general principles to their real, actual lives. When I preach, I make sure to end with some sort of application that people can take with them and apply what I just taught to their lives. As hard as I try though, I am simply unable to consider every single person's different life situation.

Verbal instruction to large groups of people is not meant to address specifics, but the specifics are what most people need.

This is why every follower of Jesus should strive to be imitated. Imitation is not just for the super Christians out there. It is not prideful to call people to copy your way of life if your life is truly lived like Jesus. If there was a human copy machine that could replicate people, would your neighborhood or church be better off if there were fifty more of you in the world?

If you've been following Jesus for any length of time, *your life should be worth imitating.* That's not self-righteous, it's just natural. I've been a pilot for over a decade. When I first started out, I was just trying not to die. Now, I spend most of my time teaching other pilots how to improve their skills. I've moved from being a nervous, unsure, inexperienced pilot to an instructor of other pilots. As I pilot, I have the self-awareness to know that the way I fly is worthy of imitation. I know my skills, I know my attention to detail, and I know that the way I do things is a great way of doing things which has been formed over years of trial and error. Younger pilots would do well to imitate the way I do things. I know this about myself. I'm not being prideful here; I'm just experiencing the natural progression of maturity.

This same attitude should be adopted in the family of God. To grow in maturity means to become increasingly worthy of imitation. This is a blessing to the people around you because more than a forty-five-minute monologue sermon on the importance of being generous with money, people need real-life examples of faithful men and women being generous with their possessions in their actual, lived lives. Being an example worthy of imitation is to bring abstract, general theological principles down from the atmosphere and onto the ground for people where they can actually relate to them.

I can't tell you the topic of the most recent sermon I listened to. I do remember with specific vividness what God taught me through my friend Eric with the peanut butter cup that one afternoon. *Discipleship is mostly caught, not taught.*

I hope you're starting to see why the *order* of our faithfulness matters. We will be unable to devote our lives to each other if we don't first devote our lives to God. By centering the name of Jesus in our own lives, we become more like him. Precious in the sight of the Lord is the death of his saints.

Our committed faithfulness to Jesus first will make us worthy of imitation. Your life is the best sermon out there because it's *real.* There are a countless number of believers coming up behind you that need you to show them what it's like to be faithfully committed to Christ.

They don't need the latest podcast about some abstract theological principle.

They don't need to listen to the most recent celebrity pastor.

They don't need to hear the most powerful new worship song.

They need you—the real you living your real life following your real Savior. This all begins with your personal, faithful pursuit of God.

Jesus taught us how to pray. In Matthew 6, Jesus provided a template we can copy and reproduce in our own prayers. He led off his prayer with an earnest request to keep God's name holy. The way we live our lives should teach others how to do just that.

How do I keep God's name holy as a parent with a full-time job?

How do I elevate the name of Jesus as a single woman longing to be married?

How do I center the worship of God when the doctor tells me that the cancer is terminal?

How do I devote myself to following Jesus when everyone around me is doubting or leaving him?

The answers to these questions are not found in a book. Your specific situation will probably not be addressed in next Sunday's sermon. No, these answers are going to come from *you and your example of faithfulness to Jesus.*

We reap the benefits of God's faithfulness to himself. Access to God's compassion, grace, slowness of anger and loyal love is ours because of God's faithful commitment to himself above all things. Likewise in the family of God, we reap the benefits of each individual's faithfulness to God.

My wife is blessed when I love Jesus more than her.

My children are blessed when I devote my first waking minutes to prayer instead of them.

My church is blessed when I take periodic breaks from pastoral ministry in order to spend time in solitude with the LORD.

Faithfulness to others begins with faithfulness to God. Let your life mirror the faithfulness of God by rightly ordering what you are faithful to. Seek Jesus first, and everything else will come in time.

❦

I preached my very first sermon at the funeral for my mother. A few days before the funeral, I woke up at two in the morning with Psalm 116:15 (ESV) on my mind:

> *Precious in the sight of the Lord*
> *is the death of his saints.*

A bold verse to preach on a day normally reserved for grief and mourning.

How could that possibly be? What is it about the death of a disciple of Jesus that is *precious* to God? Wasn't death a byproduct of sin? Death was never the plan, so why is it *precious* to God?

The death and resurrection of the follower of Jesus is the period on the end of God's faithfulness. Our old lives were bound to Jesus' in his death and because he rose back to life, so will we (Romans 6:3-5). Jesus' faithfulness transcends death and makes our resurrection possible. Every person who through faith in Christ triumphs over death is a boast for God's faithfulness. As a child of God, you are a walking taunt in the face of death (1 Corinthians 15:55).

Our death and resurrection is a victory for God's faithfulness. All the hurt, all the pain, all the doubt will vaporize instantly underneath the light of Christ. We will realize his faithfulness.

Everything he promised will come true. He will have proven himself faithful.

So believe me when I say that death is not a tragedy in the eyes of God. It's a victory for his faithfulness.

My mother loved to sing. On sunny Saturday mornings, I can remember her shouting praises along with the radio in the middle of our living room, the sun cascading down through the windows all around her. She didn't care who was watching; she paid no attention to all the pressing needs of the day. She would just sing.

She spent her life singing, so I felt it was only fitting that I would sing her out of this life and into her eternal dwelling with her Jesus.

I made the decision to take her off life support. As the nurses disconnected all her lines and silenced the alarms on her monitors, I knelt down beside her bedside and sang to her, just like she did with me.

As I sang, the alarms on her monitors kept going off as if to warn me about her fast-approaching death. The tones were incessant, as if to say "Don't you get what's happening here? She's dying! Do something!"

I could have done something. I could have ordered her back on life support. I could have prolonged her suffering in hopes of a miraculous recovery. But I didn't. Do you know why?

Because God is faithful. He will finish what he started. I didn't need to fear her death because Jesus defeated death on the cross.

Because he rose again, so will Mama.

The last song I sang her was the classic hymn *Great Is Thy Faithfulness.* I can remember my phone trembling in my hand, the lyrics hard to see through the constant stream of tears. I chose to sing that because it was the realest thing I felt in the moment. His faithfulness really is great. It's so great that not even death can overcome it. It's so boundless that it secures eternal life for those who trust in Jesus. It's so vast that it even eclipses our periods of unbelief. It's so strong that even when we doubt him, he doesn't doubt his commitment to us. Paul comforts his spiritual son Timothy with these words in 2 Timothy 2:13:

> *If we are unfaithful,*
>
> *he remains faithful,*
>
> *for he cannot deny who he is.*

I can't deny being 6'7". I can't deny being right-handed. I can't deny having a heart that beats around 100,000 times per day. God can't deny being faithful. It runs *that* deep for him.

After my mother passed, it was time to leave. I took the elevator down to the lobby to take a minute alone. I passed through the automatic doors and stepped outside into the cool, sunny, August morning. I felt the sun warm my face, the quiet of the morning comforting me. I had just experienced one of the worst moments of my life and here was this beautiful day existing just outside the concrete walls of the hospital where my mom just died. The contrast between death and life was so intense in that moment.

The sun was shining on the morning of August 13, 2018. It

felt wrong. I couldn't shake this nagging feeling. How could that day be so beautiful yet so painful? Why is the sun shining on such a dark day? This bitter, cold day doesn't deserve these sweet, warm rays of sunshine. Doesn't the sun know that I'm in mourning? Didn't it get the memo that this was a day for clouds and rain? Like the bland hospital cafe burrito I ate in silence with my dad in the basement as my mother slowly lost her vitality two floors above us, the sun just seemed out of place for the moment for no other reason that the moment was just, well, the wrong time.

The sun met my tear-stained face exactly where I was that day. It paid no attention to my current situation, it was always shining, always there. I just had to step outside to feel it.

Friends, this is exactly how God's faithfulness operates. It's not achieved through good behavior. It doesn't ebb and flow with our emotions. It's not dependent on what we feel or what we know. At some point it is simply incomprehensible. At some point we need to stop trying to figure it out. At some point we just need to leave the cold, stale hospital and

step outside,

    close our eyes,

        feel the sun on our face,

           and realize

                that it was always shining.

PART THREE

TOGETHER

I pray that they will all be one, just as you and I are one—as you are in me, Father, and I am in you.

And may they be in us so that the world will believe you sent me.

(JOHN 17:21)

CHAPTER 11

FAMILY

ONE DOES NOT simply make sourdough bread.

A few years ago, my wife picked up the hobby of making sourdough bread. When she first told me of her intentions to start making homemade bread, I was supportive but disinterested. If I were to pick up a brand-new hobby, it would be something complicated and challenging like unicycling or glass blowing or building the Death Star out of LEGOs.

But bread-making? I mean, how hard can it be?

I have never been more wrong. Making sourdough bread is a labor of love requiring patience, skill, and a whole lot of finesse. It's incredible, watching her start up another batch of dough. She transforms into Walter White tying up her apron, pulling out a kitchen scale and measuring out exact amounts of sourdough starter (a complicated process in itself), flour, salt, and water. After letting the dough rest, stretching, folding, and stretching it again, she throws it in the oven and poof!—out comes a heavenly smelling loaf of golden-brown bread.

The ingredients for sourdough are simple. The process is not.

The *process* is what transforms the basic kitchen staples of starter, flour, salt, and water into magic. There's a specific recipe that needs to be followed. Certain steps need to happen in a certain order, with specific quantities, times, and temperatures that need to be obeyed. It doesn't matter if you simply possess the ingredients for sourdough; *what matters is what you do with them.*

This is where we are at in our journey together of knowing Jesus through knowing his people. We've defined the basic ingredients to experience deep relationship with God. These ingredients are supplied by devotion to the family of God.

It's in the family of God that we learn what it means to extend and receive compassion as we vulnerably share our hurt with others.

The family of God provides opportunity to be people of grace as we learn to forgive and be forgiven.

It's by living deeply with other believers that we learn to slow our anger down by releasing and processing our anger with God and others.

By choosing to bind ourselves to a group of people over a long period of time, we can mirror what the Bible calls *hesed* or the loyal love of God through the ups and downs of relationship.

Finally, as we commit to being faithful to God first, we become more like Jesus, which is ultimately what our neighbor needs from us. The faithfulness of God to himself is our greatest good.

Likewise, our personal faithfulness to God is our neighbor's greatest need.

Compassion, grace, slowness of anger, loyal love, and faithfulness. These are the foundational ingredients for experienced relationship with God. But just like with sourdough bread, what makes these ingredients shine is not simply that we know *about* them, but what we will *do with them*.

I don't care if I have flour in my pantry. I want bread.

I don't care if I learned some interesting new way to understand God's character. I want to experience God's character for myself.

It's time to cook, y'all.

This chapter is the most exciting for me to write because we're now at our end goal: *knowing Jesus through experiencing him.* Building a nice, happy group of people who love each other is beautiful, but it's like making bread dough and serving it to your family. They'll just look at you wondering why you didn't bake it. The ultimate goal for all this is to *experience Jesus in a way that will change your life.* We want relationship with God himself, after all. Nothing less will do.

If you can remember back to Chapter 4, I said there would be a quiz later on in this book. The time has come for this quiz.

DO NOT TURN BACK TO CHAPTER FOUR, YOU CHEATERS.

I told you to remember a specific definition of our "bridge" from knowing things about God to experiencing them in real life. Ringing any bells? Well, if you're totally lost right now, I forgive you. I'll even make this quiz multiple choice to help you out.

Question: Back in Chapter 4, how did Matt define the "bridge" that takes us from knowing things about God to experiencing them?

A. Listening to "Jesus is My Friend" by Sonseed for two hours straight

B. Rewatching season one of *Veggie Tales*

C. Personal commitment to a small group of united people who are focused on living like the family of God

D. All of the above

The answer is C. I will also accept D.

God has given you his family as an incredible gift. The family of God is our on-ramp to experiencing the attributes of God on a personal level in a way that provides us with small, everyday experiences of the great things of God. By experiencing compassion, grace, slowness of anger, loyal love, and faithfulness *within* the family of God, we have something to reference here in our real lives which will open the door to know and experience these things from *God himself.* God wants us to experience his character. The church is the training ground for this.

The reason many of us struggle with a flat relationship with God is that we have settled for a flat, dull, lifeless relationship with his people. If we just show up on Sunday morning, sing a few songs, listen to a few words, and then leave, is it any surprise that our relationship with our creator suffers when we struggle to relate to the people he has surrounded us with?

One of the most popular ways the Bible describes the people of God is that of a *family*. The reason the Bible does this is that this metaphor is readily accessible to most people, and it carries massive implications if really thought out. God's people as a family is not some cute slogan from the Holy Spirit. *It's the actual intention of God.*

Take a look at these passages in Scripture that highlight God's people as *family:*

> *So now you Gentiles are no longer strangers and foreigners. You are citizens along with all of God's holy people. You are members of God's family.* (Ephesians 2:19)

> *See how very much our Father loves us, for he calls us his children, and that is what we are! But the people who belong to this world don't recognize that we are God's children because they don't know him.* (1 John 3:1)

> *Therefore, whenever we have the opportunity, we should do good to everyone—especially to those in the family of faith.* (Galatians 6:10)

> *Never speak harshly to an older man, but appeal to him respectfully as you would to your own father. Talk to younger men as you would to your own brothers. Treat older women as you would your mother, and treat younger women with all purity as you would your own sisters.* (1 Timothy 5:1-2)

Get the point? God's intentions for redeeming his people is that they would become a family. A real, messy, beautiful family. Whether it's a formal group like a small group at church or on campus, or an informal gathering of friends, most of us are already living intentionally with a group of people either inside or outside the church.

But are you family? Family is a complicated word, with lots of different meanings based off of lots of different perspectives and experiences. For our discussion, we will look to Jesus and his definition of what makes up his family.

In John 17, we see Jesus defining his family. Here we find Jesus praying for three different people: himself (1-5), his disciples (6-19), and for the church that will be built after his disciples (20-26). We are going to focus in on John 17:20-23 because it contains some vital truths we need to know about how we are to live as the family of God. Here it is:

> I am praying not only for these disciples but also for all who will ever believe in me through their message. I pray that they will all be one, just as you and I are one—as you are in me, Father, and I am in you. And may they be in us so that the world will believe you sent me.
>
> I have given them the glory you gave me, so they may be one as we are one. I am in them and you are in me. May they experience such perfect unity that the world will know that you sent me and that you love them as much as you love me.

These three verses are a *prayer* of Jesus. Let that sink in. God is praying to God.

If you're like me, you pray only when you really need something. I won't pray for my kid to get over their cold, but I will pray as hard as I can if they ever develop cancer. True, honest prayer is where our highest intentions are revealed, where are deepest desires are voiced. Our truest selves are revealed during these times of prayer.

So what's telling here is not just *what* Jesus prayed, but *that he prayed.* When you read the verses above, know that Jesus isn't praying them like you do before your $1.99 slice of Costco pizza. This isn't some little formality to take care of prior to his death. Jesus is praying with an incredible longing here with a fervency that's more like praying for someone to be healed of their terminal cancer.

Picture Jesus in a small room with his closest friends, fighting back the tears he will shed soon in the Garden of Gethsemane. Hear the longing in his voice, the strained pleading for his people to be united after he goes away. With that in mind, reread the passage:

> *I am praying not only for these disciples but also for all who will ever believe in me through their message. I pray that they will all be one, just as you and I are one—as you are in me, Father, and I am in you. And may they be in us so that the world will believe you sent me.*
>
> *I have given them the glory you gave me, so they may be one as we are one. I am in them and you are in me. May they experience such perfect unity that the world will know that you sent me and that you love them as much as you love me.*

In these three verses, we get the curtain pulled back on the highest intention and desire for the family of God. From Jesus' prayer above, we can pull out three *movements* that he desires:

1. God's people united with him (21)
2. God's people united with each other (22)
3. The world coming to knowledge of Jesus through the unity of the Church (23)

These movements are general and kind of vague. To help us practically, we will define specific *commitments* that will help us fulfill each movement. The *movements* are the desires of Christ for the family of God; the *commitments* are what the family of God dedicates themselves to in order to move in each direction.

The family of God should move *up* in their worship to a holy God.

The family of God should move *in* toward their fellow brothers and sisters in Christ.

The family of God should move *out* as they display the character of God to the world.

Many churches have already adopted this three-sided understanding of mission. Traditionally, churches offer things like Bible studies, small groups, and outreach teams (your church might use different names) for individuals to get involved with. In general, Bible studies focus on acquiring knowledge of God (up), small groups exist to foster relationship (in), and outreach groups make it their goal to love and serve those outside the church (out).

There's nothing wrong with any of this, but I see a possible opportunity here to live more in line with the family Jesus describes in John 17. What if we got rid of the individual expressions of up, in and out, and instead focused on cultivating communities of people who *do all of them together, like the family Jesus defines for us?*

The reason I feel so strongly about this is because the three movements of Jesus don't exist in a vacuum. When a singular movement is focused on, it should boost the other two.

Our pursuit of God should drive us to love other followers of Jesus (in) and serve the world (out).

Devotion to the people of God should challenge us to know God more (up) and obey Jesus together (out).

Serving the world with the love of Jesus requires us to draw strength by pursuing God (up) and spending time with the family of God (in).

Everything is connected because family is connected. As a dad, if I just focused on knowing facts about my kids without spending any time with them, you would call me a deadbeat dad. And you'd be right. If I spent all my time doing fun things with them without an interest in what was going on in their mental, emotional, or spiritual lives, I'd be missing the mark. And finally, if I focused all my energy on serving other kids in the neighborhood that needed a father figure while neglecting my own, that would be a tragedy as well. *Jesus' vision for family is a people who pursue all three movements together in a regular rhythm, letting each movement feed the others.*

So let's cast a vision for a whole, vibrant, flourishing family of Jesus. A family that *together*, moves up in worship to God the father, in with devotion to one another, and out to the world with the healing love of Jesus. All this with the ultimate goal of knowing God himself and bringing a tangible experience of God to the world.

Let's dive into the first movement, the upwards movement of devotion to God.

The LORD's prayer is Jesus' MasterClass on what's truly important. In five verses, we see what Jesus chooses to be at the top of his prayer list, and at the top of the top, he reveals what that is: *God's holiness* (Matthew 6:9).

Before any asking, before thanksgiving, before any words of lament or praise, there is this simple statement: *God, may your name be kept holy.* May it be kept holy by your people, by your creation. May you be treated as separate, as other, as *holy*.

In my opinion, there's a whole lot of encouragement out there to devote yourself to God. Today, Christian culture has resurged spiritual formation with a lot of focus on rediscovering the ancient spiritual disciplines as a way to experience spiritual growth (prayer, fasting, worship, etc.). I'm all for the spiritual disciplines, but I wonder if we are missing a step before we commit ourselves to *do* anything.

When Moses approached the burning bush in Exodus 3, one would have thought our loving and gracious God would have welcomed Moses into his presence with open arms. The opposite is actually true. As Moses got closer to the manifested presence of God in the burning bush, God told Moses to *stop coming closer to him.* He then instructed Moses to take off his sandals as a sign of reverence for the holy ground he was standing on.

Before Moses *did* anything, God held him back. God did this because he is *holy.* We, like Moses, do not get to rush into the presence of the Uncreated One. While it is true that today, we commune with God through the blood of Jesus, God is no less holy in the year 2025 than he was back on Mount Sinai with Moses.

The Hebrew word for *holy* used in Exodus 3:5 is *qodesh (ko-desh)* and one of its fundamental definitions is *set apart.* God is wholly other, on another dimension from the humans and reality he created. We can emphasize God's holy *otherness* broadly in two ways: relational and moral. God is *relationally* separate in that he shares very little in common with the physical world he created (including us), and he is *morally* separate in that he is perfect, without sin or flaws of any kind (unlike us).

So with us and God, we aren't comparing apples to oranges here. We are comparing an apple to the quantum field theory (QFT). If you're unfamiliar with QFT, it's a theoretical way of understanding quantum mechanics that combines field theory with the principle of relativity. QFT is used in particle physics and condensed matter physics to build models of subatomic particles and quasiparticles which helps to explain why the whole construct of reality is a thing in the first place.

If you have no idea what you just read, that's the point.

I am convinced, and I believe the Bible suggests, that for as much head knowledge we may collect about God, *we are barely scratching the surface of who exactly we are dealing with.* God is *holy*, he is completely *other*—and even that is an understatement. It doesn't matter if you just found out about Jesus five minutes ago, or if you hold a PhD in Systematic Theology. We all vastly underestimate the majesty, power, and *holiness* of God.

Even as that is true, God still invites us to approach him, to learn from him, and to experience him. The two primary ways he calls us to encounter his holiness is through the regular reading of Scripture and through prayer. In his kindness, God has made his very presence, his way of thinking, and his plans for us and the world accessible through his written word and prayer.

The first movement of the spiritual family of God is upwards in our worship to a holy God. The first commitment that each individual member of the family should dedicate themselves to is *the regular reading of Scripture and prayer in community.*

If we are to act like the family of God, we need to be continually immersed in the word of God. I can't emphasize this enough. If we don't do this, we will end up defining the family of God based on what feels right instead of how the Bible defines the family of God. Right knowledge leads to right experience, which leads to right action. We get the definition of what is good, true, and right from the pages of Scripture.

You probably belong to a church with a great pastor who has the gift of teaching. If that's you, praise God. The gift of teaching is given to certain people by God to shepherd his church, and good teachers are a vital part of the body of Christ. There are boundaries, though.

I'll give you $10 if you know what this word means: premastication.

Anyone out there? No? Premastication is the process some animals use to feed their young who can't chew food yet. It's commonly associated with birds who will partially digest food and regurgitate it for their young so they can eat it. The adult bird finds the food, chews the food, and throws the food up for their young to hungrily gobble it up.

Your pastor is gifted, but they're not meant to be the adult bird in this situation. Pastors are given the gift of teaching to build up the church *into maturity*, which means the longer you sit under their teaching, the less and less you'll need them to "chew" on the scriptures for you. The greatest gift you can give your pastor is to grow up, leave the nest, and be able to nourish others with the word of God on your own.

There is no substitute for direct, regular interaction with the word of God in community. Devotion to the scriptures (not your pastor's gift of teaching) is actually how Jesus defines who is a real disciple in John 8:31-32:

> *Jesus said to the people who believed in him, "You are truly my disciples if you remain faithful to my teachings. And you will know the truth, and the truth will set you free."*

The family of God is defined by faithfulness to the teachings of Jesus (God) in the Bible. An easy way to practice this in community is by using a reading plan that the entire family of God commits to. There are a ton of options out there, each with different emphasis. Our house church family has been using a two-year reading plan, with reading assignments Monday through Friday, leaving the weekends free. This pace has been pretty manageable for most people.

Regular, communal reading of Scripture is not meant to be just a box to check off to pat ourselves on the back. Engaging with Scripture is the blazing center of the unity of the family of God. By committing to reading the Bible together, we take in the necessary nutrition to grow in our maturity in Christ.

Equally important to saturating ourselves with God's word is the regular discipline of prayer. We simply cannot do anything apart from regular communion with Jesus. It's by abiding in him, by communing with his presence that we produce the results of a life lived close to Jesus. If you think about it, prayer is how we can treat God as holy, as other. We can't see God, we rarely feel him or hear him speak audibly, but we still pray. Prayer is the paramount act of faith. Do you believe God is holy? Prove it by praying.

Jesus prayed that God's name would be kept holy.

By centering the word of God in the family of God, we can be the answer to that prayer. A commitment to the scriptures and to the discipline of prayer keeps God and his name at the center of his family.

The first movement of the family of God is upwards in worship to God himself. By making our first focus, our highest desire, the holiness of the name of God, we obey Jesus' desire that his people would be in union with God. The practical commitment to this movement is the whole family of God dedicating themselves to regularly engaging with the word of God. This devotion to the word of God proves that we are the genuine family of Jesus who actually looks and acts like him.

And who benefits from a church that regularly saturates themselves with the scriptures and holds reverence for God?

The first beneficiary is the Church family itself. We have arrived at our second movement—inwards toward the other people in our spiritual families.

I am not good at holding my breath. The first few seconds are great, but then things start to get hard. Lightheadedness sets in, the face turns red, the desire for sweet, fresh air becomes intense. We humans were not meant to hold our breath.

Neither is the family of God.

The breathing pattern of the Church is to inhale communion with God and exhale love for one another. Our pursuit of God should drive us to love other people. Any theology is only as good as it leads to the love of other people (Romans 13:8). Jesus prays for more than a church who just stares up into the heavens all the time. He desires for his church to let his love motivate love for each other.

The second movement of the family of God is inward focused, on the fellow people that make up the body of Christ. For me personally, this was the hardest movement to get on board with. It seems self-centered, and in a world that has no problem prioritizing individual people over God, it seems off. Keep God at the center? No brainer. Be the hands and feet of Jesus to people who don't know him? Great idea. But to focus time, energy, and love on people who are *already in the Church*? I'm not so sure about that...

Back in John 17, Jesus makes it clear that part of his desire for the church includes unity among its family members. This unity that he desires is *real unity*, and we get the definition of this unity from, you guessed it, the Bible. In 1 Corinthians 12, we read Paul describing followers of Jesus as a body. This comparison carries strong overtones of unity, codependency, and equality among all the people who make up the Church family.

Do me a favor and look to your left. Are you aware of all the processes that needed to take place in order for you to just do that? Your lungs have been working for the last hour inhaling oxygen for your blood to transport to the cells of your muscles that just rotated your neck. Your neck muscles have been standing by, waiting for instructions from your brain to activate. The energy you used to move came from the food you ate which was processed by the stomach and transferred to your blood supply that is cycled throughout your body by your heart, which has been continuously beating, keeping you alive and able to look to the left.

Your body is an interdependent system made up of components that vary in function, but they all serve the same purpose: life. So it is with the family of God. While we may have different roles to play in the body of Christ, but they are all the same in their end purpose: *love.*

We can summarize the flow of compassion, grace, slowness of anger, loyal love, and faithfulness as *love*. Real love includes all these attributes moving around freely in a family. Love is the highest goal. At the end of it all, after all the Bible study, all the praying, all the faithful church attendance, all the singing, all the serving, *are you becoming a person of love?*

That's the ultimate question. Love is the ultimate indicator of a follower of Jesus. Read John 13:33-35:

> *Dear children, I will be with you only a little longer. And as I told the Jewish leaders, you will search for me, but you can't come where I am going. So now I am giving you a new commandment: Love each other. Just as I have loved you, you should love each other. Your love for one another will prove to the world that you are my disciples.*

It can't be clearer than that. The love we demonstrate to people *inside* the family of God will prove that we are followers of Jesus to people *outside* the family of God. Jesus could have picked literally anything else, like number of people witnessed to, size of church, number of Instagram followers, or amount of worship albums sold to equate to following Jesus. But no. He chose one thing: *love of the family of God.*

This challenges the Christian habit of releasing effort after we introduce someone to Jesus and they accept him. Many of us feel that saving faith in Jesus is like the end zone in football. Once the touchdown is scored, once a person is brought to the goal line of salvation, the work stops. Nothing could be further from the truth. The mission of Jesus is *just beginning* once faith in him is professed. The long obedience to Jesus is the main struggle most people will face. Living a life of faith is much harder than professing it.

This is why Jesus is emphasizing this love within the church so much. Truly living for Jesus is hard. We need the family of God to love us into continued faith in Jesus. I hope you're starting to see why this inward movement is incredibly important for the continued life of the church. We will wither and die alone. The love of the family of God is what keeps us going. We love the family of God by choosing to live out the character of God. We love one another by choosing...

> *compassion over ignorance,*
>
> *grace over judgment,*
>
> *slowness of anger over quick frustration,*
>
> *loyal love over fleeting interest,*
>
> *and faithfulness over self-centeredness.*

The commitment for this inwards movement toward one another is *personal devotion to a small group of people who are focusing on living like the family of Jesus.*

You are unable to love a thousand different people. You can't even truly love one hundred people to the level Jesus desires you to love them. Probably not even fifty. Or thirty.

Loving people requires time and sacrifice, both of which are in limited supply. This is why the commitment to small families is vital if we are to move toward the family of God in unity. You may have thousands of people at your church, but the family of God you are devoted to must be small.

In my experience, once a family reaches around fifteen people, it becomes increasingly hard for love for one another to flow with the strength it needs to keep the family in union. Think of it like water flowing through a garden hose. The longer the hose, the weaker the water pressure. The more people in a single family unit, the less strength is available to push compassion, grace, slowness of anger, loyal love, and faithfulness around to all its members. Sure, you'll get a trickle of compassion here, a couple drops of faithfulness there, but over time, the family of God will weaken and die off due to lack of love.

If our experience inside the Church with relationships is largely flat, shallow, or lifeless, it could be because we are casting too wide a net for relationship. If we feel pressure to know and pursue every person we come across, we'll end up pursuing no one while feeling alone, guilty, and stuck. We were not created for a family level of unity with hundreds or thousands of other people. It might feel safer to have shallow relationships with lots of people instead of deep, vulnerable relationships with a few. However intimidating that feels, God designed us to best fit into small families of people.

We've been throwing around the word *devotion* for a while, and I'd like to unpack that for a minute. While it might sound magical to be involved with small family of Christ followers who love you and love Jesus, it's not as picturesque as you might think. For this to work, every single member of the family of God must be devoted to living like the family of God.

I've met so many people who are down with the *idea* of living like family, but when it comes to actually committing to doing the hard, long-term work of family life, they resist. Real, raw, biblically defined family is nothing like a daytime movie on the Hallmark channel. It requires intense commitment and radical self-sacrifice. It's hard, but it's so worth it. Shout out to all the math nerds out there, devotion to the family of God looks like this:

Devotion = (Pursuit + Vulnerability + Accountability) / Time

Everyone in the family of God must be in *pursuit* of God and each other. Many of us are used to a "top-down" model of church with a few leaders responsible for everyone else. These "super Christians" faithfully lead others in worship to God as well as ministry to the rest of the church. Over time, church can start to feel more like a zoo, where people can go to watch the really spiritual people worship and minister. This should not be so.

In a true family of God, every single member has the responsibility to initiate relationship. Every single week should include some sort of pursuing activity, whether it's sending a quick text after you've prayed for someone, setting up a time to meet and talk about life, or actually meeting together to encourage one another. This pursuit happens outside of the family's regular rhythms of meeting, including Sunday morning. Everyone pursuing everyone.

Vulnerability is the practice of making known the hard parts of life. The pain and sin we carry must be exposed to others for it to be healed. Back in the chapter on compassion, we discovered that without vulnerability, compassion can't exist. Vulnerability is hard but necessary for true family.

The family of God who commits to being open, honest, real, and raw with their hurt and sin will experience the compassion of each other, which will point to the compassion of God. Again, this is not just for the mature members of the family.

Every single person should aim to be growing in their capacity for vulnerability as hurt and sin are safely and privately confessed inside the family. In our church family, the men and women of the church meet separately twice per month to abide in Jesus and pray, but also to confess sin, reveal hidden pain, ask for forgiveness, and receive compassion. It's a beautiful thing to be a part of.

The final ingredient for devotion is *accountability*. This is the practice of being able to give and receive correction. Accountability is absolutely necessary in the family of God. There is a high standard to live up to if you call yourself a follower of Jesus. Where there is trust, the family of God has the unique opportunity to be able to challenge, correct, and speak truth in love with a spirit of gentleness (Galatians 6:1).

When I first heard myself leading worship, I was appalled at how horrible I sounded. This was because up until that point, I had only heard my voice in my own head. I needed an outside reference of my voice to accurately determine how good (or bad) it actually was. The same goes for us as followers of Jesus. We need an outside reference (another person) to help us accurately view ourselves. We might think we are patient, loving, or generous when in reality, we might not be any of those things. We are terrible judges of our own character.

So if you have friends that love you, praise God. If you have friends that you are able to be vulnerable with, praise God. But if those friends don't have the freedom to hold you accountable for your actions and call you out on your mistakes, they are just friends, not family. There is a difference between friends being devoted only to your happiness versus devoted to your growth in Christ. Spiritual families are made up of the latter.

Accountability in the family of God helps us to rightly view ourselves. By allowing others to gently confront and challenge us, we grow in spiritual maturity. If we surround ourselves only with people who affirm our every action, we will fall. Iron sharpens iron (Proverbs 27:17).

All of this takes *time*. Over months and years of practicing pursuit, vulnerability, and accountability, the devotion that each member brings to the family of God will start to create a sacred, holy intimacy with other believers. A new spiritual family will be born. Spiritual families are not born on Sundays. They are born out of many small, seemingly mundane experiences that over time, combine to create something incredible.

A true family of God loves one another. This love is motivated by the love that God shows us, which we experience as we are faithful to him first. By *devoting* ourselves to a small group of people who are committed to doing the hard work of living like family, we practice giving and receiving the love of Christ. But this love is not meant to stay inside the church. God's love flowing through a spiritual family is meant to crest and spill over its banks, out onto the whole of God's creation, bringing vibrant renewal and refreshment to those around us (John 7:38).

I've seen people experience personal revival as a result of being a part of a true spiritual family. But it's so much more than that. When the Church of Jesus actually lives like the family of Jesus, there are massive implications for the *world* as well.

This is the third movement of the family of God: *outward to the world.*

Toward the end of his time on earth, Jesus gathered his disciples to give them final instructions for what to do next after he leaves. We read what Jesus told them in Matthew 28:18-20:

> *Jesus came and told his disciples, "I have been given all authority in heaven and on earth. Therefore, go and make disciples of all the nations, baptizing them in the name of the Father and the Son and the Holy Spirit. Teach these new disciples to obey all the commands I have given you. And be sure of this: I am with you always, even to the end of the age."*

Jesus makes it clear here, he has the authority. Because of his death and resurrection, Jesus submits to no one. Rather, all creation submits to him. From this position of authority, he commands his disciples to go out into the whole world and teach people to obey everything he has said. Jesus wants his disciples to replicate themselves.

One of your titles as a follower of Jesus is *priest* (1 Pet. 2:9). In the Old Testament, the priest was the "connector" between the people and God. He was the representative of God to the people, and the representative of the people to God. Through the priest, the presence of God was mediated (connected) from heaven to earth.

The priests oversaw worship, sacrifice, obedience to the law, and the general spiritual welfare of the people. Since we are priests serving underneath the High Priest of Jesus, our relationship to the world reflects the priests of the Old Testament. We are called by Jesus to mediate his presence here on earth. We do this by going out into the world and bringing the Kingdom of God to earth. The church is a community of priests, all working together to bring the Kingdom of God to earth, reconciling people with their creator. Where the Kingdom of God is, there is righteousness, joy, and peace. As priests, this is our driving motivation for serving the world, to bring creation back into a place of wholeness or *shalom* with its creator.

Our last movement of a family of God is outward into the world. To accomplish this, the commitment that each member of the family should adopt is to *live like missionaries in their own context.*

Bringing God's Kingdom to earth requires us to live like missionaries. This doesn't mean you need to move to some third-world country. Some are called to that, but for the rest of us, we are called to serve in our immediate contexts. Our context will be determined by our life stages, family situations, work demands, and passions/interests. There is no right way to be a missionary, and there are no mission fields more important than others. For those of you who have no idea where to begin with this, I would suggest you first look toward your passions, interests, or desires. Some of us might have a desire to come alongside single mothers, others might be drawn to those recovering from addiction or youth from hard places. Find what interests you, or what type of person really pulls on your heart and start there.

Life stage is another factor to consider. Those of us with young kids might want to consider what opportunities already exist in your community to serve others with young kids. If you find yourself living in a big house in the suburbs, perhaps God is calling you to stay in your development and show radical hospitality to people who often move to the suburbs to have privacy. The possibilities are endless. Get creative, have fun, be bold, make mistakes, and do it all in the name of Jesus.

As a missionary, your first goal shouldn't be to get your unbelieving friends into your church auditorium to experience the compelling music and listen to a dynamic speaker. Your goal should be to get people to experience the unity and love of your small spiritual family. Jesus was clear about this in John 17. They need to see *a family*. Maybe in your backyard with your spiritual family, with the kids running wild and forgotten hamburgers getting too well done on the grill.

Maybe the first worship music they should hear should be some Christian hip-hop coming out of a portable speaker as people stand around eating off paper plates and getting food stains on their clothes.

Maybe the first sermon they hear shouldn't be from a person on a stage but from a group of friends around a campfire, telling stories of Jesus' faithfulness in between sarcastic jokes and full-bellied laughs.

Maybe family has been the way forward for the Church all along, and maybe *you* are the exact person God is calling to participate in one.

Whatever church setting you find yourself in, you can cultivate a spiritual family *right now, where you are.* You can be a part of a spiritual family that mirrors the character of God for the flourishing of the Church and the salvation of the world. With a group of like-minded brothers and sisters in Christ, you can fight for and display the unity that will cause the world to be reconciled to its creator.

You are the person the Church is waiting for. You are the person Jesus is calling to help lead his Church. You are the exact person we need to show others the love of the family of God. You don't need a seminary degree. You don't need to be a talented speaker. You don't need to be a Bible scholar. You don't need to have a massive following. You just need *love*. Love for Jesus and for his people.

God desires the church to be the place where his character is not just taught, but *experienced*. He does this by calling his people to live like family. In a true, biblical family of God, compassion, grace, slowness of anger, loyal love, and faithfulness will flow freely. They will be experienced by those outside the family of God. God wants to be experienced and he has chosen the Church to be the vehicle for that experience. Here is the John 17 prayer of Jesus once more, this time in the CSB:

> *May they all be one, as you, Father, are in me and I am in you. May they also be in us, so that the world may believe you sent me. I have given them the glory you have given me, so that they may be one as we are one. I am in them and you are in me, so that they may be made completely one, that the world may know you have sent me and have loved them as you have loved me.*

The *union* of God's people will bring others into *union with God*.

How's that for an evangelism strategy? The real reason the world will be convinced that Jesus is God's son is by the *unity of the church*. The world won't be saved because of a charismatic preacher. It won't be convinced by a great apologist. It won't be moved into obedience to Jesus by the latest mass-produced worship album. The masses of people currently lost without Jesus will not be won back to him by theological intelligence alone. No, God's *big dream* is to use *small families* of people to bring his creation back to true knowledge of him.

When people encounter the *family* of God,

displaying the *character* of God,

they will come to *know* God.[4]

---

4   For a practical, down-to-earth example of how our church family has chosen to live intentionally together, check out the appendix at the back of this book.

LYRICS

IT WAS ABOUT two in the morning, and I was somewhere over the Rocky Mountains. I had just finished up a four-day rotation as an airline pilot and I was heading home from Los Angeles on the redeye to Minneapolis. A cramped middle seat near the bathrooms is no place to get some rest so I resigned myself to another sleepless night and started browsing the seat back entertainment system for something good to pass the time.

I like to think of myself as an amateur rock and roll historian so you can imagine my excitement when I came upon *Bohemian Rhapsody*, the 2018 drama about the rock band *Queen* and their flamboyant and complicated lead singer, Freddie Mercury. Excited by my finding, I pressed play and settled into my economy seat to enjoy the next few hours until I touched down back home.

My favorite scene from that movie was about the creation of the famous arena-rock anthem, *We Will Rock You*. The band (minus Freddie) was sitting around in a recording studio looking bored, waiting for their often-late lead singer to show up. As the frustration mounts, the lead guitarist (Brian May) calls the band up onto the little stage in the studio. He then recounts their most recent concert and how the audience was singing their songs back to them. It was a magical, surreal experience. Hearing tens of thousands of people singing in unison, the concert seemed to transcend what was possible with music, and it all started with involving the audience in the performance.

With that in mind, Brian has an idea. What if the band wrote a song that invited the audience to join in? What if, even for just one song, the band wasn't just the four musicians on stage, but thousands upon thousands of people in the audience as well? What could the audience do to participate? He then instructs the rest of the band in a simple progression:

Stomp. Stomp. Clap.

Stomp. Stomp. Clap.

The band follows along, looking a bit skeptical. This is Brian's great idea? Stomp, stomp, clap? It's so simple, it feels childish. Certainly not quite the fit for one of the greatest rock bands of all time.

As the band continues to comically run through the progression, Freddie decides to show up. Like the rest of the band, he looks confused watching his friends hammer out such a simple beat using their feet and hands. Suspiciously, Freddie questions Brian about this new, strange beat they were producing. Brian tells Freddie that he wants to give the audience a song that they can perform, something that will make them feel a part of the band. They can't play instruments, nor can they all come up on stage and sing. So what can they do?

They can stomp, and they can clap.

It's simple enough for one person to do, yet powerful enough that when thousands of people do it in unison, magic happens.

Freddie, still not completely convinced, allows them to continue and slowly warms to the idea. As the band continues to stomp and clap, the excitement and possibility build. Freddie sees the potential. It's genius. It's so simple, yet so powerful. He turns to Brian, and with a wry smile on his face, asks the question:

What's the lyric?

⌇

Your life is meant to be a song.

That doesn't mean you should walk around audibly singing all the time. I'm sure you have a great voice when you're belting it out in the privacy of your car. I just ordered a cup of Guatemala dark roast from my local coffee shop and if I ordered it by singing to the barista, there would be questions.

Like great music, the way you live your life should *affect* other people. It should move them to feel something profound. Your entire life, from the way you treat your own family, to the level of frustration you feel when wronged, your attitude about work, to how you handle disappointment speaks much more loudly than anything you say. *Your life is a song.*

In 1 Peter 2:9 (ESV), we hear Peter encouraging us to view the entire family of God as a united, singular unit. As a result of that, we have a collective response as the Church.

> *But you are a chosen race, a royal priesthood, a holy nation, a people for his possession, so that you may proclaim the praises of the one who called you out of darkness into his marvelous light.*

Peter calls all of us who follow Jesus a distinctly chosen, holy, and beloved people for God's own possession. What greater honor is there? But notice the response to all that at the end. Since we are God's own people, we are to *proclaim the praises* of him.

That's the song our lives must sing.

God did not save us so we can sit back, relax, and just watch life go by. We have a job to do here on this earth; we have a specific song to sing with our lives. Everything we do must proclaim the praises of God. We must show, with our lives, what makes God glorious, worthy of praise and adoration.

And we can't sing about something (or in this case, someone) *we don't know.* If we don't have a real, actual relationship with Jesus, our song will make no sense to us, or to the world.

In middle school, I was given the opportunity to join the school band. As fate would have it, I was assigned to the trumpet. I hated that trumpet. While the jocks with girlfriends were busy hammering away on percussion or tuba, I was stuck awkwardly among the trumpets, my 6'4" frame laboriously blowing into that cursed brass instrument, the bane of my existence. I sounded like Donald Duck being strangled.

I haven't totally processed the trauma of playing trumpet. Thanks for listening.

I was so bad, but I was also a genius. Who is going to know if, during our band practices and concerts, *I just faked it?* There were about twelve trumpets in our section. If I could just master *looking like I played trumpet,* wouldn't that be enough? No one would find out. Brilliant.

So that's what I did. For every practice and concert, I put my lips on the mouthpiece, pretended to blow, and fingered the notes as if I was actually playing. For the most part it worked, except when I had solo assignments to perform for the director. I would just do my best for those and accept the consequences later. It didn't matter in my mind. I was satisfied with *appearing* to be a trumpet player, instead of being an *actual* musician.

Can you see where I'm going with this?

Our lives should be a song of praise to God. We know this. The problem is that over time, the lyrics to the song we are supposed to sing have become fuzzy. What happened to those happy, early years with Jesus when we belted out his praises freely and effortlessly? Life happened. A million little distractions, a thousand good things, and a few hard things stole our singing voices.

We know the song; we've just forgotten how to sing it.

So what's the song we're supposed to sing? When God puts his ear to our lives, what should he hear? What are the praises we are to proclaim? It's great to have a general beat and rhythm driving our lives. Stomp, stomp, clap is a good start.

Now what's the *lyric*?

In verse one, our lives should sing of God's *compassion*. By suffering with other people in their hurt and pain, our lives show the world that God does the same for us. God isn't simply aware of our pain, he voluntarily suffers with us.

Verse two is all about the *graciousness* of God. Our lives should sing about God's great grace toward us by showing great grace toward others. Being a gracious person is to resolve to continually give others the gift of forgiveness, even when we don't feel like it and even when they don't deserve it. Just like God.

The decrescendo occurs in verse three, where we shift to singing about God's *slowness of anger*. God's anger is slow and focused on restoring relationship, not punishment. By committing to be angry with others in this way, our lives sing of a God whose anger is actually meant to bring us closer together.

We bring the volume back up in verse four as we sing about God's *loyal love*. So far, this song seems so wonderful that it defies logic. That's because it is. God, through his Son, has bound himself to us. We have the opportunity to sing about this indescribable love by choosing to bind ourselves to each other, no matter the cost.

The song reaches its apex in verse five. This verse is what ties the rest of the song together because it's about God's *faithfulness*. God is always true to himself. He never acts out of character. As a result, we can trust that the first four verses will always be true. By committing our lives to God first, we can sing the song of his faithfulness as the people around us benefit from our pursuit of God alone above everything else.

This is why God is worthy of praise. This is what we should praise him for.

These are the lyrics to the song our lives should sing. And in God's family, the song will be led by *everyone.*

The next revival of the church will not be televised. It will not be led by charismatic preachers who draw thousands to hear them speak. It will not be driven by highly produced gatherings and big budgets. It won't be built on the attractive persona of any one leader. It will not be loud and visible.

It will begin softly and quietly, like snow falling in the middle of the night.

It will start with early morning prayer meetings with a friend, by the tired, hushed voices praying simple prayers. It will be fueled by lots of small, everyday encounters with God and with each other. By watching each other's kids, by sharing frozen pizza in a crowded dining room, by sitting silently with a brother or sister to just hold space for grief. It will be carried along through the beautiful mundane of everyday life, with joyful celebrations of God's provision, and tearful hugs of confession and forgiveness.

Its soundtrack will not be highly produced and polished corporate worship music but the yearning, hungry voices of ten friends with a guitar in a secluded basement, singing until their voices give out or the guitar strings break. The sounds of revival will come from the simple ones with their untrained voices crying out to God without regard for what they sound like.

It will be built not by attractive, charismatic, talented leaders but by the normal, everyday, holy-yet-sometimes-messy disciples of Jesus. The kind of people who really try to love Jesus well but who aren't afraid to admit that they don't have it all together. The people who, with sometimes quivering voices, encourage and teach others not with the authority of a seminary degree but by the power of the Holy Spirit, who gives them the words to say in the moment they need them.

The next revival of the Church will be powered by the Holy Spirit using stay-at-home parents, minimum-wage workers, former drug addicts, convicted felons, students at college campuses, old saints at the sunsets of their lives, and people from every socio-economic background. God will use the forgotten, cast aside, and disregarded of the world to bring revival to his world.

The song of revival will be sung by *everyone*, not just those who are "in the band."

Stomp, stomp, clap.

God has given you his people as an incredible gift. It's by living deeply with the family of God that we can tangibly experience the very things God wants us to know about himself. By devoting ourselves to God's people we can learn the lyrics of the song God is singing *to us* and the song he wants us to sing *to the world*. Recovering what it truly means to *know God* will lead to unstoppable revival first in our own hearts, and in the world.

Yes, Lord. Let it be so in this day, in this hour. Let this generation be the one to recover the whole meaning of knowing you, with all of our minds and all of our hearts. Give us fresh experiences of your love, your majesty, and your glory as we pursue union with your people. May we all be one, as you are one with the Father. Do it in our time, in our church, in our nation, in our world. We plead with you Lord, give us a vision and a desire to love one another with all the intentionality, endurance, and devotion you desire for your Church until you come again. Amen.

The time for reading this book has ended, the time for responding to its message has come.

In John 17:3, Jesus prayed for you. He prayed that you would know him. To know Jesus is to experience him, and he has given you relationship with his family as a means for that experience. There is a deeper life with Jesus than the one you are currently experiencing. This life comes through loving the family of God and allowing yourself to be loved by them. Love is the song that is sung by those who know God.

So find your people,

make a home,

and start singing.

HOME CHURCH RULE OF LIFE

Our church family adopts what's called a *Rule of Life*. A rule of life is a set of practices that a community adopts to guide them into pursuing Christ both individually and collectively. Christians around the world have used this tool of discipleship for thousands of years to create and define communities of faith centered on the spiritual disciplines in an effort to grow together into greater Christlikeness.

These seven practices are the commitments that our community has adopted as we strive to move inward, upward, and outward as a family of God. They are what we ask everyone who calls us family to work toward in their own lives. Your specific context will be different, so your specific practices may be different which is just fine. The goal is, as it has always been, to grow together to become more like Jesus.

Monthly Commitments

1. Attend men's or women's discipleship nights (every other week) where the focus is on abiding with Jesus in prayer, being vulnerable with how life is going, confessing sins, and ministering to one another

2. Live like a missionary in your own context by serving those who don't know Jesus through acts of service, with a special emphasis on your own neighborhood, the poor, or those in distress/trial

3. Commit to regular prayer for our spiritual family throughout the month (1-3 days per month)

Weekly Commitments

1. Attend a weekly prayer and worship gathering focusing on musical worship, teaching one another from the Bible reading plan, and sharing a meal together

2. Regularly meet with other members of the family each week for prayer, encouragement, Bible study, a meal, to serve together, or just to have fun

Daily Commitments

1. Follow our daily Bible reading plan (two-year plan, averages two to four chapters per day, Monday through Friday)

2. Devote time each day for personal prayer

Whatever the vision is for your own spiritual family, I pray that God would richly bless you with a deeper knowledge of him through relationship with his people. If you're feeling the desire to work this out in your own context with your own people, check out The Union Community section on page 285.

The Author (L) and Charles Barkley (R)

A NOTE FROM MATT

Thanks for reading this. No really, I am so honored that you chose to spend your time with me on this journey of knowing God.

I'll get to the point: I am a no-name house church pastor and wannabe Christian author with no social media presence. If you found this book to be even remotely helpful, it would mean the world to me if you left a review on Amazon and shared this book on your social media channels. I have chosen not to pursue traditional publishing strategies in favor of a more underground, organic method of marketing. *You* are my marketing strategy.

I hope you'll consider helping me expand the reach of this book. No action is too small, from mentioning it to a friend, posting a picture/review on your social channels, leaving an honest review on Amazon, or just setting this book out on your coffee table (the cover is pretty, right?).

I'd be eternally grateful if you'd consider partnering with me to get this thing off the ground. To God be all the glory.

THE UNION COMMUNITY

This book is useless unless the principles inside it are applied in real, actual faith communities.

It sounds simple, but forming genuine Christian community is *hard*. In my own experience, I've greatly benefited from people who have gone before me in this area.

If you're feeling crazy enough to practice what's in this book with your own church small group, on your college or high school campus, or among your specific group of friends, I'd love to be your biggest supporter.

The Union Community is a network of small groups that have decided to relentlessly pursue living like family in their own contexts. It's a place to grow, be encouraged, share struggles, and dream of a future that makes obedience to the commandment of Jesus to love one another central.

Whether you're feeling the call to start your own family of faith or take your existing community to a more intentional level, I want to hear your heart, ideas, and dreams. Writing a book is fun, but walking alongside and encouraging other followers of Jesus is what I love the most.

Visit *www.mattbradway.com* and scroll down to The Union Community section to learn more. It's all free. Let's find a time to chat and we can figure this out together.

THANK YOU

Thank you Jesus for your love. I hope that I have brought you joy and honor by writing this book. To you be the glory in the church throughout all generations, forever and ever. Amen.

Thank you Becca for your love, support, honesty, and encouragement. You make me a better man, and your tenacious love for other people is inspiring to me. Love you, girl. Brunch is on me next Friday.

Thank you Nora, Hallie, and Caleb for letting dad spend time writing. Your lives have given me great joy. I am called a lot of things in this life, but my most prized title is being your dad.

Thank you David for lending me your artistic expertise and believing in this project. But most of all, thank you for being a great friend. Love you man. Nouvelle next week?

Thank you Abbey for editing this book. You were blunt enough to keep me honest, and encouraging enough to keep me going. Let's do another one someday.

Thank you Becca and Erin for being my ruthless beta-readers. You made this book so much better. I am humbled at your generous gifts of time and heart.

Thank you Corner Coffee—Northeast for the immaculate vibes as I wrote this book. Also, thanks for the free refills and for asking me how the writing was going every Friday morning.

Thank you to all the guys at Metro Hope for all you've taught me. God is still writing your stories. Keep staying desperate for Jesus, keep singing.

Thank you Eric for all the ways you have shown me the love of Jesus. I am following you as you follow Christ. Also, thanks for the peanut butter cup that one day.

Thank you Noah for your example of how to live a life faithful to Jesus. I watch how you live and I am challenged to be a better husband, father, and friend. You are one of the great men in my life.

Thank you to the entire Morrison family for your love and friendship. You truly are the best neighbors ever. Please don't ever stop randomly inviting us over for weeknight dessert.

Thank you to the Irving and Farwell house churches for being the hands and feet of Jesus so many times for our family and to our North Minneapolis neighborhood. I love you all.

Finally, thank you to all the guys at Farwell Church. Pastor Noah, J-Mart, Kyle the Realtor, Big Dawg, Triple-B, and Young Jacques. We've laughed, wept, and fought together because we are real brothers in Christ. You guys have shown me compassion, grace, slowness of anger, loyal love, and faithfulness. I am thankful to God that I get to call you my brothers.

ABOUT THE AUTHOR

Matt Bradway is a house church pastor and air ambulance pilot living in Minneapolis, Minnesota. He is the author of zero best sellers and pastors a dynamic, rapidly-growing house church network boasting an average weekend attendance of 20-30 people.

He got his college degree entirely online and graduated middle of his class from Ms. Betty's Sunday school class of 1995.

He enjoys good coffee, bad thunderstorms, and the sweet, promising air of sunny mornings in early June.

This is his very first book.

To say hello, invite Matt to speak, or pretty much anything else, please visit www.mattbradway.com

For a collection of teachings from Matt, visit his YouTube channel at www.youtube.com/@mattbradway

www.ingramcontent.com/pod-product-compliance
Lightning Source LLC
Chambersburg PA
CBHW021708120626
46545CB00004B/1458